EZRA AND ESTHER

Commentaries by Cyril J. Barber
Published by Wipf and Stock

Joshua: "We Will Serve the Lord"
Judges: A Narrative of God's Power
Ruth: A Story of God's Grace
*First Samuel: The Sovereignty of God
Illustrated in the Lives of Samuel, Saul, and David*
*Second Samuel: The Sovereignty of God
Illustrated in the Life of David*
*The Books of Kings, 2 Vols.
The Righteousness of God Illustrated in the Lives
of the People of Israel and Judah*
Ezra and Esther

* * *

Commentaries Published by
Christian Focus, Ross-shire, Scotland

Nehemiah: The Dynamics of Effective Leadership
1 Chronicles: God's Faithfulness to the People of Judah
1 Chronicles: God's Blessing of His Faithful People

EZRA AND ESTHER

A Devotional Commentary

Cyril J. Barber

Wipf & Stock
PUBLISHERS
Eugene, Oregon

Quotations marked NASB are from the *New American Standard Bible*, copyrighted 1960, 1962, 1963, 1971, 1972, 1973, 1975, 1977, 1995 by the Lockman Foundation, and are used by permission of the Lockman Foundation.

Quotations marked NIV are from the *Holy Bible, New International Version*, copyrighted 1973, 1978, 1984 by the International Bible Society, and are used by permission of Zondervan Bible Publishers.

Other quotations and/or paraphrases of Scripture are the author's.

Wipf and Stock Publishers
199 W 8th Ave, Suite 3
Eugene, OR 97401

Ezra and Esther
A Devotional Commentary
By Barber, Cyril J.
Copyright©2007 by Barber, Cyril J.
ISBN 13: 978-1-55635-598-1
ISBN 10: 1-55635-598-X
Publication date 8/28/2007

For...

JONATHAN

THE AUTHOR

Cyril J. Barber, D.Litt., D.Min., D.D., is pastor emeritus, Plymouth Church, Whittier, California. He has authored commentaries on the historical books of the Old Testament (Joshua through 2 Chronicles) as well as Nehemiah, Jonah and Nahum, and Habakkuk and Zephaniah. He makes his home in Hacienda Heights, California.

CONTENTS

PREFACE

THE BOOK OF EZRA
   INTRODUCTION
   PART I
1. A SURPRISING TURN OF EVENTS   1
2. THE RESTORATION OF THE REMNANT   17
3. THE TEMPTATION TO COMPROMISE   27
4. CONTINUING OPPOSITION   37
5. REVIVAL OF SPIRITUAL FERVOR   49
6. RETURN AND RENEWAL   61
   PART II
7. THE SECOND RETURN OF THE EXILES   71
8. VALIANT FOR TRUTH   83

THE BOOK OF ESTHER
   INTRODUCTION
   PART I
9. THE ROYAL BANQUET, 1:1–22   107
10. THE ROYAL WEDDING, 2:1-18   117
11. THE ROYAL VIZIER, 3:1-15   127
   PART II
12. THE QUEEN'S INTERVENTION   139
13. THE UNRAVELING OF HAMAN'S PLAN   151
   PART III
14. THE DELIVERANCE OF GOD'S PEOPLE   163

PREFACE

I am grateful for the many friends God has given me. I am particularly thankful for the help and encouragement they have been to me as I have worked on this book. To list them all would not be possible (and if I inadvertently overlooked someone I might alienate a person whose friendship means a great deal to me).

It would be remiss of me not to mention two people who worked on the manuscript. They are Maurice Bickley and David Cahn. Their help has been invaluable, and I want to acknowledge my indebtedness to them.

Ezra does not rank high among the "must read" books of our generation, but that does not excuse our neglect of it. God the Holy Spirit inspired it, and it most assuredly falls into the category of those referred to by the apostle Paul in Romans 15:4.

May the Lord use this brief explanation of it for His glory!

INTRODUCTION

Why Was the Exile of God's People Necessary?

We all have our favorite Bible stories. There are the well-known ones of Joshua and the Israelites at the battle of Jericho, David killing Goliath, Jonah and the "whale," and many more. And in the New Testament we like to dwell on the Lord Jesus stilling the storm on the Sea of Galilee, or meeting with Nicodemus, or praying in the Garden of Gethsemane. And then there are whole chapters that have been the mainstay of those enduring the trials of life like Psalm 23 or John 14–16.

Sad to say, the books of Ezra, Nehemiah and Esther are not among our favorites, yet they are as much the product of the Holy Spirit's inspiration as the New Testament letters of Paul to the Romans, Galatians, or Hebrews. The more we study our Bibles the more we realize that some important truths of the Christian life are waiting to be uncovered in the books we treat lightly.

As we consider the first of the "post-exilic" books one of the first questions we must answer, is: Why was the exile necessary? What had God's people done to incur such punishment?

Scholars have given various reasons for God's punishment of His people. Two of them are: (1) their persistent idolatry (see Psalm 106:34-39 which describes Israel's lapse into idolatry; see also 1 Chronicles 16:26-29; Psalms 96:5; 115:1-8), and (2) their refusal to allow the land to enjoy its Sabbath rest (Exodus 23:10-11; Leviticus 25:4-5; 26:34-35, 43; 2 Chronicles 36:21). Both of these explanations are valid, and yet it seems to me that there is another more basic reason: *God's people had failed to obey His written and spoken word* (Nehemiah 9:30).

In this respect we are in a similar position today. We are guilty of dereliction of our duty where God's Word is concerned (cf. Hosea 4:6). George Barna, in *What Americans Believe,* confirms this and states that for at least three or four generations we in the United States have neglected the teaching of Scripture.[1] And even when the Bible is part of college or seminary instruction, emphasis is placed on critical matters and not on what the Bible teaches.

But why was the exile of God's people necessary? The northern kingdom of Israel had been taken into captivity by the Assyrians in 722 B.C. The southern kingdom of Judah continued until 605 B.C. when it succumbed to the first of three invasions by the Babylonians. What happened between these events? In Judah, good king Josiah (640-609

---

1. G. Barna, *What Americans Believe* (Ventura, CA: Regal, 1991), 309pp.

B.C.; 2 Kings 22:1–23:30) was intent upon a religious reformation. He believed it was the only way for his people to avoid the fate that had overtaken their northern relatives. In his zeal he even extended his crusade against idolatry into the territory formerly held by Israel. While all this was going on, Assyria was tottering to its fall. Babylon was the growing power in the region. Egypt, however, was a force to be reckoned with, and its king, Pharaoh Necho (609-594 B.C.), who had recently ascended the throne, was anxious to ensure the prosperity of his people.[2] To strengthen Assyria against the threat posed by the Babylonians, Necho marched his troops to Carchemish, a fortress city on the Euphrates River.[3] The route he took required that he and his troops travel through an extensive section of Judah's coastline.

Josiah objected to Necho's action and, with a significantly smaller force, he went to Megiddo to intercept him (2 Kings 23:29). In the ensuing battle Josiah was killed. His servants brought him back to Jerusalem, where he was buried. And so ended the reforms by which Josiah had intended to bring blessing to God's people.

---

2. Evidence of Egypt's power and desire for expansion may be gleaned from the fact that its fleet had not only sailed to all parts of the Mediterranean Sea, but had circumnavigated Africa as well. Necho viewed with dismay the growing might of Babylon, and viewed the Neo-Babylonian empire as a threat to his ambitious plans. Cf. Herodotus, *History*, IV:42.
3. *Macmillan Bible Atlas,* by Y. Aharoni and M. Avo-Yonah, 3d ed. Completely revised *by* A. F. Rainey and Z. Safrai (New York: Macmillan, 1993), 158-59, 160.

Josiah was succeeded by Jehoahaz (609 B.C.; 2 Kings 23:31-33). Though Jehoahaz was not next in line, the people liked him and made him their king. They evidently felt that he was more moral and upright than his brothers. He reigned for only three months before being deposed by Pharaoh Necho, who took him to Egypt where he died (Jeremiah 22:10).

Pharaoh Necho placed Jehoahaz's older brother, Eliakim (609-597 B.C.; 2 Kings 23:34–24:7), on the throne. He probably felt that he would be easier to control. As a perpetual reminder of his power over him, Necho changed his name to Jehoiakim. The "epitaph" given him by the biblical historian is that "He did evil in the sight of the Lord."

Jehoiakim's ambition was to build for himself stately houses of cedar (cf. Jeremiah 22:13-15). The people of Judah, however, were being taxed to such an extent that their national spirit was destroyed (cf. Isaiah 51:18; 63:5; Ezekiel 22:30). Now none could be found to revive them or halt the religious decay. With nations rising and falling all about them, all that was left to the Israelites in Judah was the belief that God would not allow them to be overrun by their enemies. Their hope was in the Temple in Jerusalem. They did not believe that God would allow it to be destroyed, and therefore concluded that they were secure. Evidence for this belief is to be found in their chant, "The Temple of the Lord, the Temple of the Lord, ..." (Jeremiah 7:4. Note the context of vv. 1-15).

The teaching of the true prophets of the Lord was drowned out by the *false* prophets of the day. Their message contradicted the word of the Lord, and because they were more numerous and held influential positions (cf. Jeremiah 28:1-17), those in authority listened to them. These false prophets told the people what they wanted to hear. Their messages are described in Scripture as "lies" and the prophets as speaking "out of their own heart."

It strikes us as strange that there would be men claiming "Elijah's mantle" (i.e., to stand in the succession of the great prophets) who were misleading God's people. Being a prophet (which involved first and foremost "telling forth the word of the Lord" and only secondarily foretelling the future) was a unique calling. Some, however, for the power it gave them claimed to speak for the Lord though He had never commissioned them. It was God's righteous prophets who described for the people their real condition. It is much the same today. Godly pastors are few[4] and are invariably denounced by others for being out of step with the times.

Long before the Israelites entered Canaan (i.e., before 1400 B.C.) they were told to exterminate all the Canaanites and destroy their high places (i.e., centers of worship; cf. Numbers 33:52). They did not do so. A careful reading of the Old Testament reveals the subtle departure of the Israelites from the Lord. They did not destroy all the people, but allowed these idolaters to live among them. Their Canaan-

---

4. Following a nationwide poll George Barna determined that 49% of pastors in the United States today do not believe that the Bible is the Word of God. Of the remaining 51% only a handful have the requisite knowledge and skill to be able to teach those in their congregations the whole counsel of God (Acts 20:27).

ite neighbors were friendly. In time this led to invitations to share in their feasts. At these feasts there was drinking and dancing and a demonstration of freedom unknown among God's people. This led eventually to religious orgies, and few of the Hebrews objected when lusty young Canaanite women invited them to join in (cf. Numbers 25:1-18; Psalm 106:28-29).

How is this spirit of compromise corrected? The answer now is the same as it was for the ancient Israelites. Truth is found in what God has chosen to reveal in His Word. If others decline to accept it and go their own way, none of us can stop them. It is incumbent upon us, however, to follow the truth that God has chosen to reveal.[5]

To turn back the tide of apostasy God graciously sent His people prophets. Their task was to turn the people back to the "old ways." One of these prophets was Jeremiah (627-574), whose ministry spanned fifty-plus years. He

---

5. We have an illustration of how to handle religious compromise in Ezra 4:1-3. There we read that when the recently repatriated Jews began building the Temple, people from Samaria came and asked if they could help. They said, "Let us build with you, *for we, like you, seek your God (Elohim); and we have been sacrificing to Him since the days of Esarhaddon king of Assyria*, who brought us up here [cf. 2 Kings 17:24-29, 33]." But Zerubbabel and Jeshua and the rest of the heads of fathers' households of Israel said to them, "You have nothing in common with us in building a house to our God (*Elohim*); but we ourselves will together build [a Temple] to *Yahweh* God of Israel, as King Cyrus, the king of Persia has commanded us."

played a prominent part in the reigns of Josiah, Jehoahaz, Jehoiakim, Jehoiachin, and Zedekiah, and his ministry to the people of Judah continued after the third deportation of his people to Babylon (586 B.C.).

When opposition to Jeremiah's ministry made it dangerous for him to walk the streets of Jerusalem, the Lord told him to write a summary of all His messages to His people. This was carried out by Jeremiah's amanuensis, a man named Baruch. He was then instructed to take the scroll and read it to the people who frequented the Temple. This came to the attention of the King Jehoiakim who commanded that the scroll be brought to him. His reaction to what he heard resulted in an attempt to destroy the Word of the Lord, for he carved up the scroll and threw the pieces into a fire that was burning in his stateroom (Jeremiah 36:22-24). Meanwhile Baruch and Jeremiah had to go into hiding.

God's sentence against Jehoiakim was befitting his many crimes (Jeremiah 36:29-31; see also 22:19). His end came when he broke his oath to Nebuchadnezzar (in favor of an alliance with Egypt). His revolt failed, and he disappears from the pages of God's Word with none to lament his passing.

During Jeremiah's period of enforced seclusion he dictated to Baruch all the words that form our present Book of Jeremiah (Jeremiah 36:32).

After Jehoiakim there was Jehoiachin (597 B.C. 2 Kings 24:8-16). Jehoiachin (also called Jeconiah and Coniah) was eighteen when he became king. His reign lasted for three months. The testimony of Scripture is that he did not learn the lessons of history but continued in the evil practices of those who had preceded him. When Nebuchadnezzar came up against Jerusalem Jehoiachin with the royal family and his officials went out and surrendered unconditionally to him.

Nebuchadnezzar took him to Babylon where he languished in prison for thirty-seven years. After Nebuchadnezzar's death Evil Merodach released him and raised him to a position of honor among the conquered monarchs (2 Kings 25:27-30; Jeremiah 28:4).

With Jehoiachin's surrender to Nebucadnezzar the first deportation of the people of Judah took place. In all 10,000 of the most powerful, intelligent, wealthy, and skilled people were taken to Babylon. The Temple and the king's residence were ransacked, and all the wealth of Jerusalem was taken to Babylon as the spoils of Nebuchadnezzar's campaign. Only the poorest of the people remained in Judah (2 Kings 24:14).

Nebuchadnezzar set on the throne of Judah a son of Josiah named Mattaniah, and he changed his name to Zedekiah (597-586; 2 Kings 24:17–25:21). The leadership vacuum in Jerusalem was filled by inexperienced individuals and Zedekiah's style of leadership made it easy for his counselors to become his masters (Jeremiah 38:5).

Unscrupulous men exploited the restlessness of the people (cf. Jeremiah 27:1-22). The tensions between true and false prophets were exacerbated whenever there was a discussion about the length of the captivity (Jeremiah 5:4-5). The false prophets said that the captivity would last for only two years (Jeremiah 24:1-10), whereas Jeremiah predicted a seventy-year captivity (Jeremiah 25:1-11). Naturally the people gave ear to the things they wanted to hear (Jeremiah 28:1-17). This made the people of Judah an easy target to those who favored revolt against Babylon through an alliance with Egypt.

Eventually Zedekiah sided with the dissidents. Once again Nebuchadnezzar invaded the land and besieged Jerusalem. The promised help from Egypt and the anti-Babylonian alliance failed to produce the desired results. After a siege of about a year and a half Jerusalem fell to the invaders. Zedekiah and his family, with his bodyguard, escaped at night and fled to the plain of Jordan. There they were captured and taken to Riblah where Zedekiah's sons were killed before him.

Certain prophecies relating to Zedekiah seemed to be contradictory (cf. Jeremiah 34:3; 2 Kings 25:7; Ezekiel 12:13). They are easy to harmonize. Zedekiah actually saw Nebuchadnezzar "eye to eye and face to face," then his eyes were put out and he was taken to Babylon in chains. He never saw the land of his captivity. After this the prophecy of Micah 3:12, uttered nearly 150 years earlier, came to pass. The city of Jerusalem and its Temple were completely destroyed.

With the death of Zedekiah's sons it seemed as if the Lord's promise to David (of an heir who would always sit on his throne) had failed. Where now was God's pledge and covenant that had been the mainstay of His people for centuries?

As we shall see, God was not outwitted. Zerubbabel was of King David's line, and he and his descendants had the right to sit on David's throne.

PART ONE

THE RETURN UNDER ZERUBBABEL

EZRA 1:1--6:22

CHAPTER ONE

A SURPRISING TURN OF EVENTS

EZRA 1:1–2:70

When I was in seminary one of our assignments was to read through the entire Bible--the Old Testament as well as the New. Some of my fellow classmates objected to having to spend time on the Old Testament. They believed that their efforts would be better spent reading the New Testament, and in particular the letters of the apostle Paul. Needless to say, they were overruled. Our professor explained that "all Scripture is inspired by God and profitable for teaching, for reproof, for correction, for training in righteousness; so that the man of God may be adequate, equipped for every good work." (2 Timothy 3:16-17). Of course, there was some grumbling. There have always been students who feel that the assignments given them are either unnecessary or unjust. The fact remains, the Bible's teaching is relevant. It reveals that the way God has worked with His people in one era of history can help us understand His dealings with us at the present time (cf. 1 Corinthians 10:11).[1]

---

1. Cf. M. Breneman, *Ezra, Nehemiah, Esther*. Vol. 10, The New American Commentary (Nashville: Broadman & Holman, 1993), 16.

Looking back, I can say that in my fifty-plus years of ministry I have found the Bible to be amazingly pertinent to our times. When interpreted correctly, principles can be found that apply to people of all ages and every period of history. And this will prove to be true in our present examination of the Book of Ezra.

Recently I had to go to a hospital for some tests. While I was there, one of the nurses shared with me a matter that was weighing heavily upon her heart. Her daughter had left home to go out into the world "to find herself." Both this nurse and her husband had pleaded with her, but to no avail. Their daughter had chosen what she believed to be the path of pleasure and satisfaction. As expected, it involved keeping company with those who were involved in alcoholism, pleasure-seeking pastimes, drugs, and sex. This mother's concerns were by no means unique. I have had to counsel numerous parents whose sons and daughters had followed a similar course of action. Now that their children have attained adulthood, many of them are thoroughly disillusioned with life and their hearts have become hardened to all that is good and right.

The few who have evidenced a desire for change have expressed their despair in words like, "I cannot go home again. I've hurt my parents too much. I've turned my back on God and I haven't been to church in years. I've broken all ten of the Commandments over and over again. How can God possibly forgive me? There's no hope for me. How can I undo what I've done?"

These individuals feel that their past deeds will not allow them to return to the Lord (cf. Hosea 4:1).[2]

We should not underestimate the difficulties facing those who belatedly wish to return to the "straight and narrow way" (Matthew 7:13-14). They are filled with recurring doubts about the Lord's willingness to forgive them; and the pull of past pleasures is at times overwhelming. In their misguided efforts at reform, they will often join a cult or theologically liberal church, believing that this religious activity will restore to them what they have lost.[3]

Jeremiah had ministered to the people of Judah, but his counsel had been uniformly rejected (cf. Jeremiah 23:9-22, 25). The *false* prophets claimed that the exile of their countrymen would last for only two years (Jeremiah 28:3). This gave all concerned a false hope. To Jeremiah fell the difficult task of informing those in captivity that their banishment would last for seventy years (605-536 B.C.). He encouraged them to settle in the land of Babylon, build houses for themselves, plant gardens and eat the produce, marry and rear children, and seek the welfare of the city in which they lived (Jeremiah 29:1-32, noting esp. vv. 4-13). Initially, no one believed him.

---

2. The experience of those in this kind of situation is a replay of God's words through Hosea (see Hosea 4:1-3a, 6a, 10-12; 5:4, 6, 15).
3. A careful reading of the books of Hosea and Jeremiah shows only too clearly that God's ancient people trod the same path people do today. And the warning of the prophets about listening to "false prophets" is one that we need to heed.

THE RETURN OF THE EXILES UNDER ZERUBBABEL

EZRA 1:1–6:22

The Decree of Cyrus, 1:1-4

At the time of our story the seventy years had passed, but God's people had forgotten the words of Jeremiah (Jeremiah 25:11-12; 29:10). Most of them were content to live in Babylonia. They were taken up with making a living. Then, on the evening of October 12, 539 B.C. everything changed. The Medes and Persians, under the brilliant leadership of Cyrus the Great (559-530 B.C.), defeated the Babylonians.[4] To everyone's surprise the city was not looted and religious and civil institutions were left intact.

We read that in his first year Cyrus, "in order to fulfill the word of Yahweh by the mouth of Jeremiah, Yahweh stirred up the spirit of Cyrus king of Persia, so that he sent a

---

4. "The Cyrus Cylinder," *Ancient Near Eastern Texts Relating to the Old Testament*, 2d ed., ed. J. B. Pritchard (Princeton: Princeton U., 1955), 315-16; A. T. Olmstead, *History of the Persian Empire* (Chicago: Chicago U, 1948), 45-49; J. M. Cook, *The Persians* (London: Orion, 1983), 8, 16, 43-46, 60, 262.

proclamation throughout all his kingdom, and also put it in writing, saying: 'Thus says Cyrus king of Persia,

"Yahweh, the God of heaven, has given me all the kingdoms of the earth, and He has appointed me to build Him a house in Jerusalem, which is in Judah. Whoever there is among you of all His people, may his God be with him! Let him go up to Jerusalem which is in Judah, and rebuild the house of Yahweh, the God of Israel; He is the God who is in Jerusalem. And every survivor, at whatever place he may live, let the men of that place support him with silver and gold, with goods and cattle, together with a freewill offering for the house of God which is in Jerusalem."'"[5]

We note Cyrus' use of the expression, "God of heaven." It shows his respect for the God of the Jews. It is worthy of note that in the books of the Old Testament written before the exile He is referred to as "the Lord of Hosts," whereas after the exile He is spoken of as "the God of heaven"--an expression that implies that He is sovereign and therefore all-knowing and all-powerful.

The same kind of permission was given to the other nations whom Nebuchadnezzar had deported. The end of Cyrus' famous Cylinder gives the reason for the king's action. He desired the goodwill of the gods of each country. This is how his command ended: "May all the gods whom I have resettled in their sacred cities ask daily Bel and Nebo[6]

---

5. These words are identical with those that conclude 2 Chronicles. The two books are thus connected by a common link, and it is probable that Ezra also wrote 1 and 2 Chronicles.

for a long life for me and may they recommend me to him ... [the text is unclear]; to Marduk, my lord, they may say this: 'Cyrus, the king who worships you, and Cambyses, his son, ...[the text is unclear] ....'"[7]

Several statements in these verses are of importance to us. Cyrus' actions fulfilled the prophecy of Jeremiah uttered many years earlier. The people had scorned Jeremiah and listened instead to the false prophets. But what God had spoken through His prophet now came to pass. It should not surprise us that the people of Judah were swayed by these *false* prophets, for the same is true today. People will flock after those preachers who tell them what they want to hear and give little thought to the authenticity of the message that is preached (cf. 2 Timothy 4:3-4).

The edict of Cyrus would have been carried by couriers on horseback to all the provinces of Cyrus' dominion. Once in the public square of each town or city the text of the proclamation would have been shouted out to all within the sound of the envoy's voice. A copy of the edict would then have been given to a local official.

Cyrus was concerned that the temples that had been destroyed by his predecessors be rebuilt, that sacrifices be offered to the god of that place, and that prayers be offered

---

6. Babylonian gods.
7. *Ancient Near Eastern Texts*, 315. (The clay cylinder containing Cyrus' edict is 2,500 years old, and though some portions are worn to the point of being illegible it is in a remarkably good state of preservation.)

up for him and his sons. From his own words it is evident that he looked upon Yahweh, God of the Jews,[8] as a powerful *local* deity. Note his words: "He is the God who is in Jerusalem ... the house of God which is in Jerusalem ... [and give] a freewill offering for the house of God which is in Jerusalem" (1:3-5).

People have often asked if Cyrus was a believer in the one true God. Nearly two hundred years earlier Isaiah had predicted that Cyrus would initiate the restoration of the Temple (Isaiah 44:28-45:7,13). However, it is not necessary to assume from Isaiah's references that Cyrus was a true believer (note Isaiah 45:4). The famous cuneiform cylinder of Cyrus records his belief in several gods.

Preparation for the Journey, 1:5-11

Imagine the astonishment of the Jews throughout Babylonia as word of Cyrus' decree spread. Two generations in a foreign land had made many of them indifferent to the Lord and His plan for His people. They were more concerned with their comfortable lifestyle than they were of rebuilding God's Temple in Jerusalem. Others, a minority, were filled with amazement at the thought that the prophecy their parents had told them about had come true.

The renowned Bible teacher, Dr. John Kitto, wrote: "After so long an interval, very few of the original captives

---

8. Up to this point God's people had been referred to as "Hebrews." From the time of their return to Judah they were called "Jews."

would still be alive. The great body of the existing generation had been born and bred in Babylon.... As a body, they had [prospered].... They had become traders, pedlars, moneychangers, jewelers, and [clothiers]. Upon the whole, they were so comfortable and satisfied with their position, that, although unshaken in their attachment to Judaism, they felt but little disposed to forego their realized advantages, and break up their homes, to encounter the perils of the wilderness, and to undergo the privations and trials [of resettlement]."[9]

There was little to attract anyone to Jerusalem. It lay a burned, ruined heap in the midst of a desolate land. A remnant, however, chose to return to the land of their fathers. We read: "Then the heads of fathers' households of Judah and Benjamin and the priests and the Levites arose, even everyone whose spirit God had stirred to go up and rebuild the house of Yahweh which is in Jerusalem. All those about them encouraged them with articles of silver, with gold, with goods, with cattle and with valuables, aside from all that was given as a freewill offering" (1:5-6).

The emphasis in verse 4 is on the word "stirred," (see also 1:1). It indicates that the return of the exiles was the Lord's doing, and they gladly journeyed to Judah to rebuild the Temple.

For believers now there is no such hallowed place, even though some have mistakenly concluded that the church has

---

9. J. Kitto, *Daily Bible Illustrations*, 2 vols. (Grand Rapids: Kregel, 1981), I:996.

replaced the Temple. When the Lord Jesus spoke to the woman at Jacob's well He said, "an hour is coming when neither in this mountain nor in Jerusalem will you worship the Father" (John 4:21). He also stated that where two or three have gathered together in His name, there He would be in their midst (Matthew 18:20). The apostle Paul explained it this way, "your body is a Temple of the Holy Spirit who is in you, ... therefore glorify God in your body" (1 Corinthians 6:19-20).

Just as the Egyptians had given liberally to the Hebrews at the time of the Exodus, so now those in Babylonia–Jews as well as Babylonians–gave liberally for the rebuilding of the Temple and for the sacrifices that would be offered to the Lord once the altar had been erected.

Not to be outdone, King Cyrus brought out the articles of the house of Yahweh which Nebuchadnezzar had carried away from Jerusalem and put in the house of his gods, and Cyrus had Mithredath the treasurer give a full accounting to Sheshbazzar, the prince of Judah (1:7-8).

But who was Sheshbazzar? The identity of Sheshbazzar has caused a lot of confusion. Dr. Merrill F. Unger clarified the issues for us: "That Sheshbazzar and Zerubbabel are one and the same is evident from (1) his being called the "prince [*hannasi'*] of Judah" (1:8), a term marking him as head of the tribe in the Jewish sense; (2) his being characterized as 'governor' *peha*, appointed by Cyrus (as was Zerubbabel, 5:14); and yet more distinctly by the assertion (5:16) that 'Sheshbazzar came and laid the foundations of the house of God in Jerusalem,' compared with the promise to

Zerubbabel (Zech. 4:9), 'The hands of Zerubbabel have laid the foundation of this house, and his hands will finish it.'"[10]

The words "prince of Judah" give a subtle hint that even though a descendant of King David was not presently sitting on the throne of Israel, yet there was someone of royal blood who could do so.

A problem occurs when we add up the number of gold and silver vessels brought out of the temple of Nebuchadnezzar's god and find that it does not add up to the 5,400 mentioned in the biblical text. Is this evidence of an error in the Bible, or is there some plausible explanation? The problem is exacerbated because the Apocrypha (1 Esdras 2:10-14) mentions 5,469 items that were given to Sheshbazzar. Critics eagerly pounce on this supposed discrepancy, while ignoring the fact that it is common in Hebrew to give only an *excerpt* in place of all the specifics. (Differences in vocabulary may also have made translation difficult, and this may account for certain omissions in the text.)

The Remnant That Returned, 2:1-70

Dr. Harry A. Ironside reminds us that this chapter contains "a sample-page from the books of eternity; a leaf out of God's memorial record book."[11] God shows how careful He is in taking note of each individual and each family, and

---

10. M. F. Unger, *Unger's New Bible Dictionary*, ed. R. K.. Harrison (Chicago: Moody, 1988), 1181.
11. H. A. Ironside, *Notes on the Books of Ezra, Nehemiah and Esther* (Neptune, NJ: Loizeaux, 1978), 18.

the work they accomplish for Him. There is something peculiarly solemn about records like these. The people listed are not known to us, but God has not forgotten them, and in time He will reward each one according to his work (Psalm 62:12; Proverbs 24:12; 1 Corinthians 3:13-15).

Those Jews who did return to Judah were animated by strong desires to see and possess once more the land of their fathers (2:1). The majority of the 42,360 repatriates were poor as is evident from the fact that they had only 7,337 male and female servants and 6,720 donkeys. Most of the returning exiles made the journey on foot; and the 6,720 donkeys would most likely have been used for carrying food, household items, and other articles too bulky to have been carried with ease. There were also a number of horses, mules, and camels in their caravan, but these would have been insufficient for the women and children.[12]

Among those who did return were some leaders of the people (2:1-2), specific families who probably settled in Jerusalem (2:3-20), men[13] from different cities (2:21-35), priests (2:36-39), Levites (2:40-42), temple servants (2:43-54), descendants of Solomon's servants (2:55-58), and a large number of uncertain genealogy (2:59-63).

---

12. In all, there were a little more than 8,000 animals for 42,360 people besides 7,337 male and female servants, and 200 singing men and women.
13. Many of these men may have been single. This may account for the intermarriages that caused a problem later on.

More than 4,000 priests returned, but only 74 Levites. Ezekiel had censured the Levites, downgrading their function because of their sinful practices (Ezekiel 44:10-16), and this may account for their poor response. But looked at from a human point of view, they had no inheritance in Judah for the Lord was their inheritance (Deuteronomy 18:1-2). It took a genuine commitment on the part of the 74 Levites for them to leave their homes and sources of income in Babylon for an uncertain future in Judah.

The journey was made without mishap, and on arrival in Jerusalem the people gave expression to the joy that was in their hearts. Their song of praise is preserved for us in Psalm 126:1-3:

"When Yahweh brought back the captive
 ones of Zion,
We were like those who dream.
Then our mouth was filled with laughter
 And our tongue with joyful shouting;
Then they said among the nations,
 'Yahweh has done great things for them.'
Yahweh has done great things for us;
 We are glad."

This psalm of praise was later sung by pilgrims coming to Jerusalem to worship the Lord.

Included with those who willingly went to Jerusalem was a large group who could not prove their genealogy: "Now these are those who came up from Tel-melah, Tel-harsha, Cherub, Addan and Immer, but they were not able to give evidence of their fathers' households and their descendants, whether they were of Israel." Many claimed to be priests. "These sought their names among those who were registered by genealogy, but they were not found; therefore they were excluded from the priesthood as defiled" (Ezra 2:59-63).

Unfortunately there are many in Christendom today who are characterized by zeal and (at least outwardly) a desire to serve the Lord, but who are unable to give a clear answer for the hope that is in them. We need to exercise caution in passing judgment on such people, but they should not be awarded positions of responsibility in the church until there is some evidence of the work of the Spirit of God in their lives (Jude 1:4; cf. 2 Timothy 2:19).

The returning exiles gave liberally of their wealth to restore the foundation of the "house of God," support the work of the priests and Levites, and maintain the daily sacrifice. The total number of those who returned to Jerusalem is repeated in Nehemiah 7:66 (and in the Apocryphal book of 1 Esdras 5:41). The individual lists add up as follows: Ezra, 29,818; Nehemiah, 31,089; and 1 Esdras, 30,143. Critics are delighted with these totals because they appear to support their contention of errors in the Bible. It should be borne in mind that some people who signed up for the trip may have backed out at the last minute. This may have been especially true of the Levites.

The question that we must ask ourselves is this: What do we learn from these chapters?

God's Providence

The Jews had paid little attention to the predictions of God's prophets (cf. Jeremiah 29:19). In this respect they differed little from Christians today who give lip service to the Scriptures, but ignore the very principles that God has propounded that could be of such encouragement to them in times of difficulty.

Secular theorists have argued that what Cyrus did was merely a wise policy. They believe that he had perceived certain segments of the people to be languishing in poverty, and realized the mistake of keeping a disaffected population in the very heart of his empire. According to these social scientists it was a wise policy to allow these unhappy individuals to return to their native lands. But this does not take into account the prosperity of many of the formerly disenfranchised people, Jews included, who had established thriving businesses in Babylon. Nor does it take into consideration the wisdom and power of God who, after seventy years of captivity, "stirred up the spirit of Cyrus" to issue the decree of emancipation (Jeremiah 29:10).[14]

As we ponder what the Lord did for His ancient people, it fills us with wonder at His power and wisdom and timing. He who stirred up the heart of King Cyrus also stirred the

---

14. About 200 years earlier Isaiah had predicted that Cyrus would decree the liberation of captive races, including God's people (Isaiah 44:21-28; 45:1, 5). This was long before Cyrus could see the plight of captive peoples within his empire.

hearts of His people so that nearly 50,000 volunteered to go to Judah. It is part of the great revelation of God in history, that He works continuously to bring about His purposes in spite of the ignorance (and, at times, malice) of world leaders. And realizing this, we are encouraged to pray for those in authority (1 Timothy 2:1-2).

God's Possessions

The biblical historian also records the fact that Cyrus gave instructions for the sacred vessels brought to Babylon by Nebuchadnezzar be returned. Why did Cyrus do this? Whenever a temple was plundered by an invading army, the sacred treasures were placed in the temple of the god worshiped by the conqueror. It was believed that this humiliated the god of the conquered people and showed him to be powerless. Viewed in this light, the restoration of the sacred vessels of Yahweh of Hosts, appears to be more than an act of generosity. It put an end to the insult offered the God of Israel by the king of Babylon.

CHAPTER TWO

THE RESTORATION OF THE REMNANT

EZRA 3:1-13

Many a believer, as he or she looks back on the years since his/her acceptance of Christ, has to confess with the song writer:

> I've wandered far away from God,
> Now I'm coming home;
> The paths of sin too long I've trod.
> Lord, I'm coming home.[1]

But getting right with the Lord is harder than it may appear. The early joy is gone, and in its place is doubt over whether God will fully accept us. That is why this chapter from the Old Testament book of Ezra is so important, for it illustrates the process as well as what we can expect when we seek to get right with God.

We continue our perusal of the book of Ezra with the return of the exiles under Zerubbabel (1:1–6:20). The

---

1. From the hymn, "Lord, I'm Coming Home," by William James Kirkpatrick (1838-1921).

events of this chapter deal with the early construction of the Temple.

CONSTRUCTION OF THE TEMPLE, 3:1-13

The Jews had made the journey from Babylonia to Judah (about 900 miles) by following the Euphrates River to Aleppo. Then they turned south to Jerusalem.[2] The trip would have taken at least four months (cf. Ezra 7:8-9). It seems likely that the Israelites left Babylon about the Spring of the year. On their arrival at Jerusalem they found the city in ruins, and the surrounding towns and villages in a shambles. Their first thought would have been the need to construct temporary dwellings for themselves.

The Sacrifices Offered, 3:1-6.

There is evidently a gap of several months between chapters 2 and 3. During this period the Jews spent time in earnest labor building their homes and making preparations for the rebuilding of the Temple. Rubbish and the debris left by their Babylonian conqueror had to be cleared away.

Then, in the month Tishri (corresponding to our September/October) those living in the towns and villages

---

2. *Macmillan Bible Atlas*, 167.

around the Holy City came as one man to Jerusalem to celebrate the Feast of Tabernacles (Leviticus 23:39).

During the seventy years of exile it is doubtful if the Law of Moses had been taught on a consistent basis. And, of course, the regular sacrificial system had not been maintained. Now that the remnant had returned to Judah, and possibly at the urging of the priests, the people came to Jerusalem to fulfill the Law's demand.

The people could have excused themselves from attending the feast, for they had legitimate cause to fear that while they were away from their homes marauders from the surrounding countries would plunder their possessions and drive off their flocks and herds. It is to their credit that they put their relationship with the Lord ahead of all other concerns.

The sacrifices prescribed by Moses fell into two classes: (1) those offered for the sake of communion with the Lord; and (2) those offered in communion. In the first category were sacrifices for propitiation that included sin and trespass offerings. Those in the second category involve burnt offerings; peace offerings (i.e., thank offerings, votive and freewill offerings); and grain and drink offerings.

The burnt offering symbolized the entire surrender (or dedication) of the individual to the Lord. In its highest sense it looks at the Lord Jesus Himself who, as a Lamb without spot, offered Himself to God; and in a secondary sense it speaks of the believer's heartfelt dedication of himself to the will of God (Romans 12:1-2).

As the people began to gather, Jeshua and Zerubbabel (representing the religious and secular divisions of their society) set an example for the returning remnant. They arose and built the altar of the God of Israel. Everything was done according to the Law of Moses, the man of God (3:2). They realized that they were a chosen race, a royal priesthood, a Holy Nation, a people for God's own possession, and it was their duty to proclaim the excellencies of Him who had called them out of darkness into His marvelous light (cf. 1 Peter 2:9).

The people recognized the hand of God in their repatriation, and they wanted to worship Him in sincerity and truth. Their desire to honor Him, however, was mingled with fear. They were few in number when compared to their hereditary enemies (Amorites, Ammonites, Edomites, Moabites, etc.), and they were easily intimidated. These enemies had a long history of antagonism toward God's people, and the ancient animosities had not cooled during Judah's exile.

It must be borne in mind that fear arises in our hearts when we take our eyes off the Lord (cf. Peter's experience in Matthew 14:23-32, noting esp. vv. 28-30). We believe that other people or circumstances can harm us or take away our ability to function independently. The Lord Jesus taught that we should fear Him (Matthew 19:28; Luke 12:4-5); and by placing our confidence unreservedly in Him, we are kept from being controlled by our fears.

In the sight of the people, the priests offered up to the Lord a burnt offering. This was in obedience to God's

Word, but on this occasion there was no fire from heaven to consume their sacrifice as there had been when the first Temple was dedicated (cf. 2 Chronicles 7:1). However, in obedience to the Lord, from this day forward burnt offerings were sacrificed both morning and evening. This implied that the people gave themselves to the Lord as they began the day, and placed themselves in His protective care as the day came to a close.

We cannot fail to observe that in verses 4-6 there is a repeated emphasis on the place of the whole burnt offerings. When we have strayed from God's will we need not only to acknowledge our need of Him and ask Him to pardon our offenses, but we also need to rededicate ourselves to Him in complete obedience and devotion.

Next, the Jews kept the Feast of Booths (or Tabernacles, 2 Chronicles 8:13; Ezra 3:4; Zechariah 14:16,18-19). This feast was connected with the exodus of the Israelites from Egypt, and reminded the people of God's gracious protection of them throughout their wandering in the wilderness (Deuteronomy 8:7-18; cf. 3:4-6).

The Foundation Laid, 3:7-13.

The situation of the Jews in Jerusalem reminds me of a group of about sixty devout believers who wanted to build a church in which to worship. Their funds were limited to what each family could contribute; but undaunted, they gave up their weekends to clear the land. When the foundation was laid they assembled on the dried concrete, sang praises to the Lord, and dedicated to Him what they had done.[3]

But this was only the beginning. The men, with their wives and children supporting them, then began to erect the walls. It was tiring work. Each man had his regular place of employment, and the work of building the church had to be done after hours and on weekends. Another celebration was held when the building reached windowsill height. And another just before the roof capped the project.

I always looked forward to visiting this group of believers, for through their efforts they developed a love and unity that could be felt before any of the usual greetings were exchanged.

In Jerusalem, at the time of the burnt offerings, the foundation of the Temple of Yahweh had not been laid, but it soon followed. The leaders gave money to the masons and carpenters. They also gave food, drink and oil to the Sidonians and Tyrians in payment for the wood that was then shipped to Joppa (cf. 1 Kings 5:8-11) before being brought up to Jerusalem (possibly on ox-drawn carts).

Then we read that, "in the second year of their coming to the house of God at Jerusalem in the second month, Zerubbabel ... and Jeshua ... and the rest of their brothers the priests and the Levites, and *all* who came from the captivity to Jerusalem, began the work." The oversight of the building project was committed to Levites who were twenty years of age and older.

---

3. Their neighbors thought this to be hilariously funny, and did not hesitate to ridicule them!

There was unity on the part of those doing the work as is implied by the word "all" in 3:8. "Now when the builders had laid the foundation of the Temple of Yahweh, the priests stood in their apparel with trumpets, and the Levites, the sons of Asaph, with cymbals, to praise Yahweh according to the directions of King David of Israel. They sang, praising and giving thanks to Yahweh, saying, 'For He is good, for His lovingkindness is upon Israel forever.' And *all* the people shouted with a great shout when they praised Yahweh because the foundation of the house of Yahweh was laid "(cf. Psalm 136).

This was in marked contrast to the experience of the exiles when they first arrived in Babylon. Sorrow over their sin had robbed them of their joy.

By the rivers of Babylon,
There we sat down and wept,
When we remembered Zion.
Upon the willows in the midst of it
We hung our harps.
For there our captors demanded of us songs,
And our tormentors mirth, saying,
"Sing us one of the songs of Zion."

To this they replied, "How can we sing the Lord's song in a strange land" (Psalm 137:1-4).

In spite of the joy of the majority of the people in Jerusalem, some of the "the priests and Levites and heads of fathers' households, the old men who had seen the first temple, wept with a loud voice when the foundation of this house was laid before their eyes." They had been among those carried away into exile in either 597 or 586 B.C.[4] Their period of exile had lasted for 59 or 46 years, respectively. Though now old, they could still remember the glory of Solomon's Temple, and the present edifice gave no promise of equaling the former structure in magnificence. According to the Talmud, this Temple lacked five things that were in Solomon's Temple, namely, the Ark, the sacred fire, the Shekinah, the Holy Spirit, and the Urim and Thummim. Zechariah the prophet encouraged the people not to *"despise the day of small things"* (Zechariah 4:8-10, emphasis added).

In closing, we need to ask ourselves the question, What does all of this have to do with you and me?

When we try to get right with the Lord after wandering from Him, we must begin with the confession of our waywardness and the surrender of ourselves to Him.

Oh, Lord, I present myself to You;
My Will,
My Time,
My Talents,
My Tongue,
My Property,
My Reputation,
My Entire Being,

---

4. There were three deportations of the Jews to Babylon: 605, 597, and 586 B.C. The seventy years of captivity commenced with the first deportation.

To Be – and to do
Anything You require of me.
As I have given myself to You–
I am no longer my own, but I belong to You.
–Anonymous.

In our next chapter we will consider some of the detours our adversary will place in our path as he attempts to hinder the work of grace being done in our hearts.

CHAPTER THREE

THE TEMPTATION TO COMPROMISE

EZRA 4:1-5

Recently Jimmy Carter, America's 39th President (1977-1981), released a book entitled *Our Endangered Values: America's Moral Crisis.* The thrust of President Carter's approach is to be found in the early pages where he states that he has been motivated to "search for harmonious answers to most of the controversial religious and political questions [of our day]." Carter goes on to write that "it is in America's best interests" to find "harmonious answers" to today's moral dilemmas and "find as much common ground as possible."

As noble as this sounds, consensus, not truth, becomes Carter's highest virtue, and compromise becomes the order of the day. And though Carter makes much about "drawing near to Christ" at no time does he discuss Christ's own statement that "you shall know the truth, and the truth shall make you free" (John 8:32; see also John 14:23 and 1 John 5:3).

Carter expected an attack on his book, and so he quotes Matthew 7:1 (though he ignores the context). He condemns prideful behavior and stresses the need for compromise coupled with demonstrations of our care, generosity, forgiveness, and compassion.[1]

The Rejection of Help (4:1-3)

It is surprising how often temptations to compromise enter into our daily lives. In this chapter we are given an example of how to handle compromise. We read: "When the enemies of Judah and Benjamin heard that the exiles were building a Temple for Yahweh, the God of Israel, they came to Zerubbabel and to the heads of the families and said, 'Let us help you build because, like you, we seek your God and have been sacrificing to him since the time of Esarhaddon king of Assyria, who brought us here.' But Zerubbabel, Jeshua and the rest of the heads of the families of Israel answered, 'You have no part with us in building a Temple to our God. We alone will build it for Yahweh, the God of Israel, as King Cyrus, the king of Persia, commanded us.'"[2]

The request of the people in the ancient province of Samaria had the appearance of being in the best interests of both parties. "These Samaritans were largely of the same character as thousands in this day of grace who make a profession of Christianity but have never even pretended to own Christ as Lord, and who know nothing of the saving

---

1. J. Carter, *Our Endangered Values* (New York: Simon & Schuster, 2005), 212 pp.

value of His blood.... It is a sad mistake for the believer to be linked up with them in Church fellowship."[3]

The words of those from the province of Samaria sounded friendly, but something in their manner indicated that they were not to be trusted. They probably feared that with the authorization the Jews had received from Cyrus, God's people would establish a province of their own; and this would erode their power as governors in "the land beyond the River." Their request, therefore, was motivated by a desire to use their work on the Temple as a means whereby they could later influence the decisions of those in Judah.[4]

Zerubbabel and Jeshua and the leaders of the prominent families declined their offer. Though they had lived in Babylon for a long time, they were not cut off from the

---

2. We need to keep clearly in our minds the difference between the Temple in Old Testament times and the Church of the New Testament. In the Old Testament God lived in the midst of His people (Exodus 25:8; 29:45; 1 Kings 6:12-13), whereas in the New Testament each believer is indwelt by the Holy Spirit and is a part of the temple "built on the foundation of the apostles and prophets, Christ Jesus Himself being the corner stone, in whom the whole building, being fitted together, is growing into a holy temple in the Lord, in whom you also are being built together into a dwelling of God in the Spirit (cf. 1 Corinthians 3:16; 6:19 and Ephesians 2:20-22).

3. Ironside, 39.
4. J. Blenkinsopp, *Ezra-Nehemiah*, Old Testament Library (Philadelphia: Westminster, 1988), 107.

world. They knew that the people living in the province of Samaria had intermarried with the people from other countries who had been forcefully resettled there by Sargon II (722-705 B.C.). They also knew from their history that sacrifices had ceased once Jerusalem had been overthrown and the Temple burned. The fact that those in Samaria had been "sacrificing to the Lord" since the days of Esarhaddon, King of Assyria (681-669 B.C.) was sufficient to cause alarm, for the Lord had not appointed the altar at Bethel as a place for His worship.[5]

But how could Zerubbabel and the others in Jerusalem turn down the offer of those in Samaria without proper dialog and an attempt to reach a harmonious solution? The answer lies in the Scriptures. In 2 Kings 17:24-35 we read that "the [people of Samaria] made Nibhaz and Tartak [their gods]; and the Sepharvites burned their children in the fire to Adrammelech and Anammelech the gods of Sepharvaim." Those who had settled in Samaria were polytheistic. "They outwardly reverenced Yahweh and yet appointed from among themselves priests of the high places ..." (2 Kings 17:29-34). The biblical historian is very definite in his assessment of their situation: *"They feared Yahweh and served their own gods according to the custom of the nations from among whom they had been carried away into exile."*

---

5. Corroborative evidence for Esarhaddon's settlement of people in the depopulated province of Samaria may be found in *Ancient Near Eastern Texts*, 290; and D. D. Luckenbill, *Ancient Records of Assyria and Babylonia*, 2 vols. (New York: Greenwood, 1968), II:527-28.

But what does all this have to do with us?

Our society is becoming more and more secular and pluralistic, and it is expected that anyone who wants to get ahead will make certain compromises for the sake of his/her advancement. Dr. Francis Steele, at one time president of the North Africa Mission, found that he and those belonging to the mission were constantly facing issues involving cooperation with other religious groups, and there was the danger that in time they might lose their evangelical distinctives. To preserve the integrity of the work of NAM he propounded three principles that were to guide NAM's missionaries in making their decisions. They were to ask themselves ...

1. What is the goal or object of such cooperation?
2. How long will this relationship last?
3. Will such association mar my/our testimony?[6]

The hard-pressed, harassed people in Jerusalem knew that compromising the purity of their beliefs was not what God wanted. The psalmist had written:

---

6. It should be borne in mind that cooperation and compromise are not synonymous terms. To *cooperate* is to work in a helpful way with others; *compromise* involves setting aside one's values in an endeavor to reach a settlement in which each side gives up part of its demands.

> O how blessed is the man who does not walk in the
> counsel of the wicked,
> Nor stand in the path of sinners,
> Nor sit in the seat of scoffers!
> But his delight is in the law of Yahweh,
> And in His law he meditates day and night.
> He will be like a tree firmly planted by streams of water,
> Which yields its fruit in its season
> And its leaf does not wither;
> And in whatever he does, he prospers.
>
> The wicked are not so,
> But they are like chaff which the wind drives away.
> Therefore the wicked will not stand in the judgment,
> Nor sinners in the assembly of the righteous.
> For Yahweh knows the way of the righteous,
> But the way of the wicked will perish
> (Psalm 1:1-6).

The Persistence of Opposition, 4:4-5

The true aim of those in Samaria soon became apparent. "Then the peoples around them set out to discourage the people of Judah and make them afraid to go on building. They hired counselors to work against them and frustrate their plans during the entire reign of Cyrus king of Persia and down to the reign of Darius king of Persia. At the beginning of the reign of Xerxes, they lodged an accusation against the people of Judah and Jerusalem."

Verse 4 picks up the theme of opposition and introduces the following chapters where the building program of the Jews was thwarted. The mention of Darius I (521-486 B.C.), Xerxes (486-464 B.C.),[7] and Artaxerxes I (464-423) carries the reader forward to the time of Nehemiah and the building of the wall of the city.

Those in Samaria meant to "discourage" the workers. This word "discourage" literally means to cause them "to relax the hands," or "make weak the hands." And the "counselors" whom the Samaritans hired were probably Persian officials paid to thwart any tangible help that might have come from the kings who succeeded Cyrus (deceased 530 B.C.).

The plight of the Jews in Jerusalem parallels the difficulties faced by Christians today. As soon as a person gives evidence of a desire to walk with the Lord, people arise who try to get him or her to compromise the principles of godliness found in the Bible. At first, opposition takes the form of seemingly well-meaning counsel: "This religious quest you are on is fine, but you do not need to take it to extremes," or "I liked you better before you became a church-going junkie," or "Surely God doesn't expect you to spend all of your time in religious activities!" Then, if this does not work, the earnest believer may find his/her work in the place where he/she is employed obstructed and their plans maligned. Such opposition makes it difficult for a person to achieve any measure of success in his/her profession.

---

7. The Greek form of Ahasuerus.

As difficulties multiply and opposition becomes more tangible, we need the counsel of God's Word to keep us on track.[8] A careful consideration of this chapter provides some important guidelines.

First, we find that the leaders in Jerusalem were cognizant of their history. A knowledge of the past is indispensable when it comes to making wise decisions. Consider, for example, Romans 15:4 and the teaching of the Book of Proverbs, and then weigh the decisions made by those in Jerusalem. Like them, we should always persevere in doing what is right, show respect for our superiors, and do all tasks assigned to us to the best of our abilities, in spite of opposition (cf. John 16:33).

Second, by ordering our lives in accordance with the truth (John 17:17*b*), we become people of integrity (cf. Psalms 7:8-9; 15:1-5; 25:21; 26:1-12; 41:12; etc.); who can be trusted. Note, for instance, the example of godly men and women like Enoch, Joseph, Amram and Jochebed, Moses, Caleb, Joshua, Deborah, Hannah, Samuel, David ... and the list goes on and on. A careful study of the lives of each one will greatly enhance our own understanding of how to face the trials and vicissitudes of life.

Third, remember that we "must all appear before the judgment seat of Christ, so that each one may be recompensed for his deeds in the body, according to what he has

---

8. A helpful book by W. J. Bennett, *Virtues of Leadership* (Nashville: Word, 2001), 131pp. shows how others have succeeded.

done, whether good or bad" (2 Corinthians 5:10). This is too solemn a reality to be treated lightly. By setting our mind on the things above, not on the things that are on earth, we can better prepare ourselves for this event. Then, when Christ, who is our life, shall appear, we will be ready to be revealed with Him in glory (Colossians 3:2-4).

I recently attended the funeral of the husband of a member of our church. The service was well-organized, and the professional singer was excellent. Though the preacher spoke of the man who had died as being in heaven, his words lacked conviction, and there was no comfort for the bereaved in his message. And when individuals stood up to pay tribute to the deceased, they spoke of him as being in that "great boardroom in the sky," but their words gave no indication of a knowledge of salvation (cf. Jeremiah 23:21-22; Matthew 15:14). This is the inevitable result of theological and ecclesiastical compromise.

A glorious future awaits us. Even now we have the opportunity to dedicate ourselves to the Lord and then labor so as to be found pleasing in His sight (Hebrews 13:20-21).

CHAPTER FOUR

CONTINUING OPPOSITION

EZRA 4:6-24

The conflict between good and evil began when Lucifer (Satan) aspired to usurp the place of God (Isaiah 14:13-14). He and his followers were expelled from heaven, and ever since then they have opposed all that is good (Ezekiel 28:14-15; Luke 10:18).[1] This includes God's plan for the Messiah, the Lord Jesus Christ, who is destined to reign over all the kingdoms of the world.

As far as the Church is concerned, Satan's activity has been twofold. He has been behind all the *internal* problems that have taken the form of false teachings (i.e., heresies), and he has instigated *external* pressures that we identify with the persecutions that have been a part of every age. And sometimes these problems have been combined, coming from a state that had legalized some form of religion and forcefully suppressed others. And not to be overlooked are those occasions when Satan has instigated opposition to the message of the gospel for economic reasons (cf. Acts 19:27).

---

1. For a fuller discussion than is possible here, see the books by D. G. Barnhouse, *The Invisible War* (Grand Rapids: Zondervan, 1965), 288pp., and R. P. Lightner, *Angels, Satan, and Demons* (Nashville: Word, 1998), 212pp.

When we consider the opposition of those in the province of Samaria to the work of the Lord, we note that it was the direct result of the devotion of the Jews to the Lord (4:3). This antagonism continued unabated for a considerable period of time.[2] At first the northerners sought to hinder the building of the Temple, but later on their enmity became violent and resulted in the destruction of the walls of Jerusalem that were being rebuilt.

SPECIAL EMPHASES

Students of this book have found the material in this chapter confusing because it does not follow the chronology of the earlier chapters.[3]

The explanation is to be found in the *thematic* summary of the rule of the Persians over the Jews. Verses 1-5 describe events in the reign of Cyrus (559-530 B.C.). The Temple was completed after his death in 516 B.C. Verse 6

---

2. D. Kidner, in his *Ezra and Nehemiah* (Downers Grove, IL: Inter-Varsity, 1979), 48), has stated that "from this point onwards [i.e., Ezra chapter 4] to the end of Nehemiah there is conflict. Nothing that is attempted for God will now go unchallenged, and scarcely a tactic be unexplored by the opposition."
3. Cf. A. C. Hervey, *The Expositor* IV, 8 (1893), 50-63; H. G. M. Williamson, *Journal of Theological Studies* 34 (1983), 1-30.

deals with the reign of Ahasuerus (486-464 B.C.), better known by his Greek name, Xerxes. Data about him is followed by a lengthy section focusing on the correspondence of Artaxerxes I (464-424 B.C.). The chapter concludes with mention of Darius (523-487 B.C.).

Four letters are mentioned in these verses. It is possible that the writer did not have access to copies of the first two, but he does quote numbers three and four. From the contents of this correspondence we gain a clear picture of events as well as the people involved. When these letters were received in Babylon, they were translated into Persian.

The verses of this chapter, through to 6:18, are in Aramaic, the *lingua franca* of the Assyrian Empire in the 8th century B.C.[4] When these letters were received in Babylon, they were translated into Persian.

A REVIEW OF THE OPPOSITION TO THE WORK OF THE LORD
Ezra 4:6-24

As Christians we believe that if we live good lives, God will safeguard us from the kind of problems we read about

---

4. Cf. P. S. Alexander, *Journal of Semitic Studies* 23 (1978), 155-70; J. A. Fitzmyer, *Journal of Biblical Literature* 93 (1974), 201-25; D. C. Snell, *Journal for the Study of the Old Testament* 18 (1980), 32-51.

in our newspapers or watch on the evening news. The lives of devout people in both the Old and New Testaments tells us a different story. The apostle Paul wrote: "All who desire to live godly in Christ Jesus will suffer persecution. But evil men and impostors will grow worse and worse, deceiving and being deceived. But you must continue in the things which you have learned" (2 Timothy 3:12-14).

The First Two Letters, 4:6-7

The first letter took the form of a false accusation addressed to Ahasuerus (better known as Xerxes).[5]

This complaint apparently went unheeded because Xerxes had to put down a revolt in Egypt. Some writers are of the opinion that the Jews also revolted because archaeologists have shown that certain cities in Samaria and Judea were attacked at this time. There is insufficient evidence, however, to support the idea of a revolt on the part of a small group of people in Judea[6].

Some writers are of the opinion that the Jews revolted at this time, though there is insufficient evidence to support

---

5. A valid question has been raised: Why is there no mention of the reign of Cambyses (530-521 B.C.)? Different writers (including Josephus) have attempted to account for the omission by rearranging the text, but without success. See L. L. Grabbe, *Journal of Biblical Literature* 106 (1987), 231-46.
6. From the brevity of the chronicler's statement it seems evident that he did not have access to copy of this letter.

such a theory. Archaeologists have shown that certain cities in Samaria and Judea were attacked and burned by Xerxes, but there is inadequate evidence to support the idea that the Jews were involved in an uprising. It is more likely that Xerxes subdued these cities because he did not want to face opposition on his way back to Babylon.

The second letter was addressed to Artaxerxes (4:7). More information is known about its contents. "In the days of Artaxerxes also, Bishlam, Mithredath, Tabel, and the rest of their companions wrote to Artaxerxes king of Persia; and the letter was written in Aramaic script, and translated into Persian."

Apparently it, too, did not receive a reply. Artaxerxes had come to the throne after his brother had been murdered. A major concern during the first half of his rule was the Egyptian revolt that began in 460 B.C., and it seems obvious that he did not see the small number of people in Judah as a threat to his plans.

As we consider the letters sent by those in Samaria to Xerxes and Artaxerxes, respectively, we note that they contained accusations. All of us, whether in Christian ministry or following some secular pursuit, know how painful false accusations can be (cf. Psalms 35:19-20; 119:78; etc.). Though often couched in terms of loyalty to one's company or immediate superior, those who malign us hope that by putting us down they can secure their own advancement. And seldom are we given the opportunity to rebut the calumny of others. And even if the opportunity of a defense is given us, it is well nigh impossible to reverse the negative impressions created by those who were the first to gain the ear of our superiors.

The Third and Fourth Letters, 4:8-16

Later on another letter was sent to Artaxerxes. The person dictating the letter was a man named Rehum, and the one who actually put pen to parchment[7] was a scribe named Shimshai. An imposing list of officials added their names to the document. The content of the letter was a cunningly contrived, slanderous attack on those in Jerusalem. And not surprisingly, they were not given an opportunity to reply to it.

The Letter to Artaxerxes. "This is the copy of the letter which they sent to him: 'To King Artaxerxes: Your servants, the men in the region beyond the River, and now let it be known to the king, that the Jews who came up from you have come to us at Jerusalem; they are rebuilding the rebellious and evil city and are finishing the walls and repairing the foundations. Now let it be known to the king that if that city is rebuilt and the walls are finished, they will not pay tribute, custom, or toll, and it will damage the revenue of the kings. Now because we are in the service of the palace, and it is not fitting for us to see the king's dishonor, therefore we have sent and informed the king, so that a search may be made in the record books of your fathers. And you will dis-

---

7. Thousands of clay tablets have been found in Mesopotamia, and the assumption is that the letter to Artaxerxes was on clay. Scribes of the period sometimes used parchment (leather) or papyrus (cf. 6:2).

cover in the record books, and learn that that city is a rebellious city and damaging to kings and provinces, and that they have incited revolt within it in past days; therefore that city was laid waste. We inform the king that, if that city is rebuilt and the walls finished, as a result you will have no possession in the province beyond the River'" (Ezra 4:11-16).

This letter was slanderous and contained exaggerations and innuendos that those in Babylon could not possibly verify without an on sight investigation. Furthermore, those in Samaria readily supplied suggestions as to where Artaxerxes was most likely to find support for the accusations they had made. His researchers were guided away from the decree of Cyrus (kept in Ecbatana) to the wars of the Jews with the Assyrians and Babylonians. Documents pertaining to these battles were kept in either Babylon or Susa.[8]

It should be noted that in addition to the attempt of the Jews to build the Temple, they were also rebuilding the walls around the city of Jerusalem. An unwalled city was easy to plunder. Strong walls were essential if people and their property were to be protected.

The writer of this letter (and his collaborators) did not intend to focus attention on the Jews, but rather on the city of Jerusalem. They lost no time in describing it as a "rebellious and evil city." Their choice of the word "rebellious" was strategic, for the Persian Empire was plagued by rebel-

---

8. Blenkinsopp, *Ezra-Nehemiah*, 108.

lious factions, and any threat of further insurrection was sure to gain the attention of the king.

Those in Samaria then *hypothesized* that "if" the walls were rebuilt the Jews would not pay taxes. Taxes paid to the Persian treasury were in money, in kind, and a duty tax. The loss suffered by the suspension of these revenues (if real) would harm the treasury of the king.

But those in Samaria were not finished. In addition to refusing to pay taxes, they implied that if the walls were rebuilt, the people would rebel, taxes would not be paid, and such actions would put the king to shame. They also branded the Jews as enemies of the crown who supposedly were unconcerned about the king's welfare. To further ingratiate themselves into Artaxerxes' favor they offered as their reason the fact that they "ate the salt of the palace"[9] (i.e., they were on the royal payroll and therefore owed the king their loyalty).

It should be noted that while the person writing the letter made a pretense of concern for the king's honor, there was no hint of the true motives of those in Samaria.

Then they added the *coup de grace*. They claimed that if that city was rebuilt and the walls finished, Artaxerxes would have no possession in the land beyond the River.

---

9. H. C. Trumbull, *The Salt Covenant* (New York: Scribner's, 1899), 184pp. The reference here implies that they owed the king fealty, devotion, faithfulness (cf. Leviticus 2:13; Numbers 18:19; 2 Chronicles 13:5).

Such a charge was ludicrous. The little band of Jews could not pose a threat to the might of the Persian Empire. Artaxerxes, however, had to take seriously any intimation of unrest.

The Reply of Artaxerxes. "Then the king sent an answer to Rehum the commander, to Shimshai the scribe, and to the rest of their colleagues who live in Samaria and in the rest of the land beyond the River: 'Peace. And now the document which you sent to us has been translated and read before me. A decree has been issued by me, and a search has been made and it has been discovered that that city has risen up against the kings in past days, that rebellion and revolt have been perpetrated in it, that mighty kings have ruled over Jerusalem, governing all the land beyond the River, and that tribute, custom and toll were paid to them. So, now issue an order to these men to stop work, that this city may not be rebuilt until a decree is issued by me. Beware of being negligent in carrying out this matter; why should damage increase to the detriment of the kings?" (Ezra 4:17-22).

This letter raises the question, If the law of the Medes and Persians could not be altered, how could Artaxerxes issue an order for the work on the walls of Jerusalem to stop and then later commission Nehemiah to build the walls? Verse 21 contains the answer. Artaxerxes wisely left open the possibility of a later decree authorizing the rebuilding of the walls.

The "long history of revolt" on the part of the Jews brings to the fore in kaleidoscopic form centuries of Judean power from the era of David and Solomon to Hezekiah's defeat of Sennacherib. When this history was compacted, the conclusion reached implied an imminent threat to Persian hegemony.

The Response to Artaxerxes' Letter. "Then as soon as the copy of King Artaxerxes' document was read before Rehum and Shimshai the scribe and their colleagues, they went in haste to Jerusalem to the Jews and stopped them by force of arms. Then work on the house of God in Jerusalem ceased, and it was stopped until the second year of the reign of Darius king of Persia" (Ezra 4:23-24).

Josephus[10] and the writer of the Apocryphal book of 1 Esdras state that those from Samaria went to Jerusalem with horses and troops, and destroyed the work that had been done thus far. The chronicler then adds that the work on the Temple came to a standstill until the second year of Darius I, king of Persia (522-486 B.C.).

"But," we may ask, "of what value is all this to us?"

Throughout the centuries Christians have faced opposition and even martyrdom on account of their beliefs. The state (e.g., Nazism, Communism) and false ideologies (e.g., liberalism), and state churches (e.g., Roman Catholicism, Lutheranism, etc.) have persecuted evangelical believers.

What is to be the response of God's people to such opposition? The apostle Paul wrote: " I urge that entreaties

---

10. Josephus, *Antiquities of the Jews*, 11:2-29.

and prayers, petitions and thanksgiving, be made on behalf of all men, for kings and all who are in authority, *so that we may lead a tranquil and quiet life in all godliness and dignity*, for this is good and acceptable in the sight of God our Savior" (1 Timothy 2:1-3, emphasis added). But if this is not possible, then we are to endure hardship as good soldiers of Jesus Christ (2 Timothy 2:3). For "the Lord is good to those who wait for Him, to the person who seeks Him. It is good that he waits silently for the salvation of the Lord" (Lamentations 3:25-26).

CHAPTER FIVE

REVIVAL OF SPIRITUAL FERVOR

EZRA 5:1–6:22

I vividly recall a spiritual desert-like experience I had in my late teens and early twenties. My routine involved getting up at 4:00 A.M. to read my Bible and pray. Then, after breakfast, I caught a bus to work and spent the day working with cash statements and ledgers. My evenings were taken up with meetings and/or preaching. I was doing all the things the conventional wisdom of the day said was necessary for an effective spiritual life, yet I felt spiritually lethargic. Now, as I look back on those years, I realize that I was preoccupied with externals. Sound books on maintaining one's spiritual vitality had not been written, and though I continued to attend church and go through the motions of witnessing, I felt like a deflated balloon.

My experience must have been similar to the situation facing the returned exiles. Opposition from their enemies in Samaria wore down their resolve. Work on the Temple ground to a halt, and the rebuilding of the wall around Jerusalem ceased. A form of apathy prevailed. Though their authority to rebuild the Temple had come from none other than Cyrus,[1] when he was killed in battle it became easy for those in Samaria to oppose the work the Jews were doing.

The Preaching of the Prophets, 5:1-2

In chapter 5 we move forward to the reign of Darius I Hyarcanus (522-486 B.C.). The biblical writer describes the means God often uses to awaken us out of our lassitude. He sent the prophets Haggai and Zechariah to challenge the Jews to appropriate action. Haggai began his ministry on August 19, 520 B.C. by reproving the people for their laissez-faire attitude and for excusing their inactivity by saying "the time has not come ... for the House of the Lord to be rebuilt" (Haggai 1:2). Then He indicted them for their preoccupation with their own interests by asking "Is it time for you yourselves to live in paneled houses while [My] house lies desolate?" (Haggai 1:4).

On October 17, 520 B.C., the Lord, speaking through Haggai, addressed Zerubbabel and Jeshua. The subject was the issue voiced by those who, though old, still remembered the glory of Solomon's Temple. The Lord promised that He would fill with glory the House presently being built by the Jews (Haggai 2:7), and that its latter glory would be greater than its former glory (Haggai 2:9). The context of this promise refers to God shaking all nations (possibly a reference to the Tribulation period). This was followed by another promise, namely, that the "wealth of the nations"

---

1. Cyrus is usually called "king of Persia," but here he is referred to as "king of Babylon." Several inscriptions from the first year of Cyrus' reign (and before he became king of Persia) refer to him as "king of Babylon." This shows once again the accuracy of the biblical record, for Cyrus' decree was issued in the first year of his reign. See *Ancient Near Eastern Texts*, 316.

will be brought to Jerusalem (most likely a reference to the Millennium).[2]

Zerubbabel and Jeshua responded to the preaching of Haggai and Zechariah and motivated the people to show reverence for the Lord by recommencing work. The Temple was completed four years later (Haggai 1:12-14).

The Protest of the Provincial Governor, 5:3-17

We are now introduced to a man named Tattenai,[3] governor of the land beyond the Tigris and Euphrates Rivers. The early reign of Darius had been marked by numerous revolts in different parts of the empire. As a good subordinate Tattenai came to ascertain firsthand what was taking place in Jerusalem. We read: "At that time Tattenai, the governor of the region beyond the River, and Shethar-bozenai and their companions came to them [i.e., the Jews] and spoke thus to them: 'Who has commanded you to build this temple and finish this wall?'[4] Then, accordingly, we told them the names of the men who were constructing this building" (5:3-4).

Tattenai took a cautious approach to the work of the Jews and sent a letter to Darius. The questions asked by Tattenai were legitimate. The courteous answers he

---

2. Cf. Zechariah 14. See E. M. Yamauchi, *Persia and the Bible* (Grand Rapids: Baker, 1990), 155-60.
3. See A. T. Olmstead, *Journal of Near Eastern Studies* 3 (1944), 46.
4. Adeney, *Ezra and Nehemiah*, 86-89.

received from the Jews probably went a long way to assuaging his fears. He wrote to Darius, and a copy of his letter was included in the historic narrative.

To King Darius:
Peace.
The king should know that we went to the district of Judah, to the temple of the great God. The people are building it with large stones and placing the timbers in the walls. The work is being carried on with diligence and is making rapid progress under their direction. We questioned the elders and asked them, 'Who authorized you to rebuild this temple and restore this structure?' We also asked them their names, so that we could write down the names of their leaders for your information. This is the answer they gave us: 'We are the servants of the God of heaven and earth, and we are rebuilding the temple that was built many years ago, one that a great king of Israel built and finished. But because our fathers angered the God of heaven, he handed them over to Nebuchadnezzar the Chaldean, king of Babylon, who destroyed this temple and deported the people to Babylon. However, in the first year of Cyrus king of Babylon, King Cyrus issued a decree to rebuild this house of God. He even removed from the temple of Babylon the gold and silver articles of the house of God, which Nebuchadnezzar had taken from the temple in Jerusalem and brought to the temple in Babylon. Then King Cyrus gave them to a man named Sheshbazzar, whom he had appointed governor, and he told him, "Take these articles and go and deposit them in the temple in Jerusalem. And rebuild the house of God on its site." So this Sheshbazzar came and laid the foundations of the house of God in Jerusalem. From

that day to the present it has been under construction but is not yet finished."

"Now if it pleases the king, let a search be made in the royal archives of Babylon to see if King Cyrus did in fact issue a decree to rebuild this house of God in Jerusalem. Then let the king send us his decision in this matter" (5:6-17).

The Permission of the Persian King, 6:1-12

It must have taken considerable time for Darius' servants to go through the archives in Babylon, before resuming their search in Ecbatana. Finally they found the decree that Cyrus had written in 538 B.C. Dr. Charles C. Ryrie has noted that "The efficient Persian government kept its records on scrolls of papyrus or leather at *Ecbatana* (modern Hamadan on the road from Baghdad to Tehran). It was a city at 6,000 ft (1,829 meters) elevation, with a climate conducive to the preservation of scrolls."[5]

After finding Cyrus' decree, Darius responded to Tattenai's letter as follows:

"Memorandum --
"In the first year of King Cyrus, Cyrus the king issued a decree: 'Concerning the house of God at Jerusalem, let the temple, the place where sacrifices are offered, be rebuilt and let its foundations be retained, its height being 60 cubits and

---

5. C. C. Ryrie, *Ryrie Study Bible: Expanded Edition* (Chicago: Moody, 1995), 729.

its width 60 cubits; with three layers of huge stones and one layer of timbers. And let the cost be paid from the royal treasury. Also let the gold and silver utensils of the house of God, which Nebuchadnezzar took from the temple in Jerusalem and brought to Babylon, be returned and brought to their places in the temple in Jerusalem; and you shall put them in the house of God.'

"Now therefore, Tattenai, governor of the province beyond the River, Shethar-bozenai, and your colleagues, the officials of the provinces beyond the River, keep away from there. Leave this work on the house of God alone; let the governor of the Jews and the elders of the Jews rebuild this house of God on its site. Moreover, I issue a decree concerning what you are to do for these elders of Judah in the rebuilding of this house of God: the full cost is to be paid to these people from the royal treasury out of the taxes of the provinces beyond the River, and that without delay. And whatever is needed, both young bulls, rams, and lambs for a burnt offering to the God of heaven, and wheat, salt, wine, and anointing oil, as the priests in Jerusalem request, it is to be given to them daily without fail, that they may offer acceptable sacrifices to the God of heaven and pray for the life of the king and his sons.

"And I issued a decree that any man who violates this edict, a timber shall be drawn from his house and he shall be impaled on it and his house shall be made a refuse heap on account of this.

"And may the God who has caused His name to dwell there overthrow any king or people who attempts to change it, so as to destroy this house of God in Jerusalem. I, Darius, have issued this decree, let it be carried out with all diligence!"

It is evident that Darius shared the same concerns as Cyrus. He wanted his people to be content, for this would tend toward the stability of his kingdom. He was also concerned lest local deities turn against him and his sons and cause problems within his realm.

It is interesting to note Darius' concern for proper worship. Appropriate sacrifices to the different gods was important in the ancient Near East. The sacrifices were designed to placate the gods or else obtain their favor. In Judaism the sacrifices were for forgiveness of sins and were offered in honor of the One True God whom they worshiped.

The Aramaic of 6:3 presents some difficulties. Did the "foundations" need to be laid (NIV), or merely preserved?[6] Or is there a third possibility? Recent studies have shown that some important buildings in the region had more than one foundation. This lent greater stability to the structure the people were erecting.[7]

The decree of Cyrus placed emphasis on building the Temple on the same site as the former Temple. A problem

---

6. Williamson, *Ezra, Nehemiah*, 124.
7. See J. S. Wright, *The Building of the Second Temple* (London: Tyndale), 17; and F. I. Andersen, *Australian Biblical Review* 6 (1966), 232-35.

arises with the dimensions of the Temple. Solomon's Temple was ninety feet (sixty cubits) long, thirty feet (twenty cubits) wide, and forty-five (thirty cubits) high. Apparently the royal scribe in Babylon experienced some confusion over the dimensions of the Temple making it ninety feet high and ninety feet wide (cf. 1 Kings 6:2).

Zerubbabel's Temple had three layers of huge stones and one of timber, corresponding to Solomon's Temple (1 Kings 6:36). Why? Cyrus was concerned that the new Temple resemble as much as possible the one destroyed by Nebuchadnezzar. The gold and silver vessels taken away by Nebuchadnezzar agreed with the data given to Tattenai (cf. Jeremiah 27:21-22).

The command to Tattenai and his associates to "stay away" from Jerusalem[8] employed a legal term precluding any interference.

The Jews had anticipated another visit from Tattenai and may have believed that it would compel them to stop all work on the Temple. Imagine their joy when they learned of Darius' support and confirmation of the supply of all their daily needs (6:9).[9] It is remarkable how God is able to cause the wrath of His enemies to praise Him (Psalm 76:10).

---

8. F. Rundgren, *Zeitschrift fur die alttestamentliche Wissenschaft* 70 (1958), 213.
9. "Salt" in 6:9 brings to mind the phrase "salt of the covenant" (Leviticus 2:13; Numbers 18:19; 2 Chronicles 13:5) and its place in forming an enduring covenant.

Just in case anyone might be inclined to treat lightly his edict, Darius included the kind of punishment that was to me meted out to the offender (6:11). A beam was to be taken from his house, and he was to be impaled on it. In addition, his house was to become a refuse heap.[10]

The Praise of the Patriotic People, 6:13-22

Next we are given a summary statement. "Then Tattenai, governor of the region beyond the River, Shetharboznai, and their companions diligently did according to what King Darius had sent. So the elders of the Jews built, and they prospered through the prophesying of Haggai the prophet and Zechariah the son of Iddo. And they built and finished it, according to the commandment of the God of Israel, and according to the command of Cyrus, Darius, and Artaxerxes king of Persia" (6:13-14).

The whole community--encouraged by what they had seen of God's protection and provision--banded together, and the work moved steadily forward. The Temple was finished on the third day of the month of Adar, which was in the sixth year of the reign of King Darius" (6:15; i.e., on March 12, 515 B.C.). When the last stone or beam was in place, they celebrated with a special dedication. "Then the children of Israel, the priests and the Levites and the rest of

---

10. Herodotus, *History*, 3:159 records how Darius impaled 3,000 Babylonians; and the Behistun monument makes mention of the fact that Darius impaled numerous rebels (cf. J. Teixidor, *Journal of Near Eastern Studies* 37 (1978), 181-85.

the descendants of the captivity, celebrated the dedication of this house of God with joy. And they offered sacrifices at the dedication of this house of God, one hundred bulls, two hundred rams, four hundred lambs, and as a sin offering for all Israel twelve male goats, according to the number of the tribes of Israel. They assigned the priests to their divisions and the Levites to their divisions, over the service of God in Jerusalem, as it is written in the Book of Moses" (6:16-18).

On this occasion the animals sacrificed were *"for all Israel ... one for each of the tribes of Israel."* In this they showed their oneness with the ten northern tribes that had been taken into captivity by the Assyrians, some of whom had returned with the exiles from the tribes of Judah and Benjamin.

Because the Temple was essentially a place of worship it was necessary for the priests and Levites to take up their special duties. And they did so. On April 21, 515 B.C. they celebrated the Passover, "for the priests and the Levites had purified themselves together; all of them were pure. Then they slaughtered the Passover lamb for all the exiles, both for their brothers the priests and for themselves. And the sons of Israel who returned from exile and all those who had separated themselves from the impurity of the nations of the land to join them, to seek Yahweh God of Israel, ate the Passover. *And they observed the Feast of Unleavened Bread seven days with joy, for Yahweh had caused them to rejoice, and had turned the heart of the king of Assyria toward them to encourage them in the work of the house of God, the God of Israel"* (6:19-22, emphasis added).

The Passover was followed by the week-long Feast of Unleavened Bread. It was appropriate that this section should end on a note of worship, for an expression of true gratitude sprang from the hearts of the people. And all was done in accordance with the law of Moses.

As we reflect on the preaching of Haggai and Zechariah we are reminded of the fact that the Lord is Sovereign. He watches over us and we are accountable to Him. This should serve a twofold purpose: (1) Encourage preachers to deliver to the people the whole counsel of God (Acts 20:27); and (2) put their hearers in mind of their accountability to the Lord.

Work on the Temple was a matter of priority. When the people of Judah failed to put the Lord first in their lives He frustrated their plans (Haggai 1:6, 9-11). And the same is true in our lives when we fail to cultivate that closeness to the Lord that He desires (cf. Matthew 6:33; see also Leviticus 26:20; Psalm 107:33-34).

We close with the words of William Bullock. What he wrote aptly sums up the experience of the Jews as they dedicated the Temple:

> We love the place, O God,
> Wherein Your honor dwells;
> The joy of Your abode
> All earthly joy excels....
>
> The Word that tells of peace,
> Of comfort in the strife,
> And joys that never cease.

CHAPTER SIX

RETURN AND RENEWAL

EZRA 7:1-28

We now come to the second part of our story in which we are introduced to Ezra. Up until now we have been concerned with the activities of the Jews who returned to Jerusalem under Zerubbabel and Jeshua. They had been commissioned by King Cyrus to rebuild the Temple. Now, in verse 1 we are introduced to two people: A new king named Artaxerxes Longimanus (464-424 B.C.), and a priest named Ezra.

Turbulent Times

Artaxerxes was the third son of Xerxes. He was *not* next in line to inherit his father's throne, but was placed on the throne by Artabanus, who murdered Xerxes. Artaxerxes was very young when he ascended the throne, and shortly after his accession he put his older brother Darius to death; and a little later he had Artabanus (who perhaps aimed at making himself king) killed.

But all did not go well for Artaxerxes. His mother Amestris had his wife poisoned, and she, together with his sister Amytis, exerted considerable influence on him. Amestris also secretly encouraged his enemies to revolt against him. His brother, Hystaspes, who may have been satrap of Bactria at the time of Xerxes' death, rebelled. After two hard-fought battles he was deprived of his power and probably of his life. The reign of Artaxerxes was further disturbed by the revolt of Egypt in 460 B.C.,[1] and it was suppressed only after five years of strenuous fighting.

It was in the midst of all this turmoil that Artaxerxes commissioned Ezra to take a large gift to the Temple in Jerusalem. As we shall see, his visit was both political and religious. Artaxerxes needed a faithful ally in the west; and Ezra's visit, with Artaxerxes' gift for the Temple, was calculated to secure the favor of the Jews.

Enviable Ancestry

This historical data provides the backdrop for Ezra's journey to Judah. But who was Ezra? The chapter begins with his genealogy. As we shall see, he was able to trace his ancestry all the way back to Aaron: "Now after these things, in the reign of Artaxerxes king of Persia, Ezra the son of Seraiah, the son of Azariah, the son of Hilkiah, the son of Shallum, the son of Zadok, the son of Ahitub, the son of Amariah, the son of Azariah, the son of Meraioth, the son of Zerahiah, the son of Uzzi, the son of Bukki, the son of Abishua, the son of Phinehas, the son of Eleazar, the son of Aaron the chief priest--this Ezra came up from Babylon; and he was *a skilled scribe* in the Law of Moses, which Yahweh God of Israel had given. The king granted him all

---

1. Artaxerxes sent Ezra to Jerusalem in 458 B.C.

his request, according to the hand of Yahweh his God upon him" (Ezra 7:1-6, emphasis added).[2]

Notable Achievements

The Jews to this day hold Ezra in high esteem. They speak of him as a "second Moses," who led a group of expatriates from Babylon to Judea. They also credit him with the founding of the "Great Synagogue." And though he was a priest, he never attained to the position of high priest. Instead, he is most often referred to as a "scribe," a "ready scribe of the law of Moses," "a scribe of the words of the commandments of the Lord and of his statutes to Israel," and "a scribe of the law of the God of heaven" (cf. 7:6; Nehemiah 8:1; 12:26; etc.). Ezra and the young men in the scribal school he founded set an example for us in their study of God's Word (cf. Matthew 13:52).

Ezra's abiding claim to fame has to do with the Scriptures. It is believed that he gathered together the sacred writings that now comprise the Old Testament.[3] He also made copies these manuscripts and disseminated them to God's people who had been dispersed among the nations by the Assyrians and Babylonians.

---

2. K. Koch, *Journal of Semitic Studies*, 19 (1974), 173-97.
3. Certain Old Testament books had not yet been written: Ezra, Esther, Nehemiah, Malachi, possibly 1 and 2 Chronicles, and perhaps one or more of the post-exilic prophetic writings was not available to him in Babylon.

Of greatest value to us is Ezra's example of practical righteousness. The chronicler tells us that he "had set his heart to study the law of the LORD and to practice it, and to teach His statutes and ordinances in Israel" (7:10, NASB). Before he dared teach God's Word, he first prepared his heart to know what God had revealed. His study of the sacred text involved both his mind and his emotions. He did not presume to teach others before the truth of Scripture had gripped his own heart. His example is important. He might have said with Jeremiah "Your words were found and I ate them, and Your words became for me a joy and the delight of my heart" (Jeremiah 15:16). Too often today those who stand in our pulpits regurgitate material from other people's published sermons or spout data they have obtained from the Internet. It is no wonder that their ministry lacks unction and those who sit under their ministry are not fed.

Once Ezra had learned the mind and will of God, he undertook to put it into practice in his own life. He did not traffic in half-lived truths. It is easy for contemporary pastors and teachers to excuse themselves by claiming that the pressure of numerous activities does not give them much time for study. Such an excuse, however, reveals how lightly they value their calling.

All of this reminds us of the late Dr. G. Campbell Morgan who, during his lifetime, was regarded as one of the greatest preachers in the U.S. and the U.K. His daughter-in-law, Jill Morgan, wrote his biography entitled *A Man of the Word: Life of G. Campbell Morgan*. In it she mentioned how her father-in-law would never preach a sermon without reading the passage to be expounded forty or fifty times. It is no wonder that he held spellbound congregations on both sides of the Atlantic.

Royal Commission

We do not know how Ezra came to the attention of Artaxerxes. We do know that in the seventh year of his reign (459 B.C.), and in spite of the unfavorable report which had been sent to him by Rehum and Shimshai, he commissioned Ezra to go to Jerusalem. The decree gave Ezra the power to take with him a company of Israelites, together with priests, Levites, singers, porters, and Nethinim (7:7).

The king's commission was specific. The chronicler included a copy of it in this book.

"Now this is the copy of the decree which King Artaxerxes gave to Ezra the priest, the scribe, learned in the words of the commandments of Yahweh and His statutes to Israel: 'Artaxerxes, king of kings, to Ezra the priest, the scribe of the law of the God of heaven, perfect peace. And now I have issued a decree that any of the people of Israel and their priests and the Levites in my kingdom who are willing to go to Jerusalem, may go with you. Forasmuch as you are sent by the king and his seven counselors to inquire concerning Judah and Jerusalem according to the law of your God which is in your hand, and to bring the silver and gold, which the king and his counselors have freely offered to the God of Israel, whose dwelling is in Jerusalem, with all the silver and gold which you find in the whole province of Babylon, along with the freewill offering of the people and of the priests, who offered willingly for the house of their God which is in Jerusalem; with this money, therefore, you shall diligently buy bulls, rams and lambs, with their grain offerings and their drink offerings and offer them on the altar of the house of your God which is in Jerusalem. Whatever seems good to you and to your brothers to do with the rest of the silver and gold, you may do according to the will of your God. Also the utensils which are given to you for the service of the house of your God, deliver in full before the God of Jerusalem. The rest of the needs for the house of your God, for which you may have occasion to provide, provide for it from the royal treasury. I, even I, King Artaxerxes, issue a decree to all the treasurers who are in the provinces beyond the River, that whatever Ezra the priest, the scribe of the law of the God of heaven, may require of you, it shall be done diligently, even up to 100 talents of silver, 100 kors of wheat, 100 baths of wine, 100 baths of oil, and salt as needed. Whatever is commanded by the God of heaven, let it be done with zeal for the house of the God of heaven, so that there will not be wrath against the kingdom of the king and his sons. We also inform you that it is not allowed to impose tax, tribute or toll on any of the priests, Levites, singers, doorkeepers, Nethinim or servants of this house of God.

"You, Ezra, according to the wisdom of your God which is in your hand, appoint magistrates and judges that they may judge all the people who are in the province beyond the River, even all those who know the laws of your God; and you may teach anyone who is ignorant of them. Whoever will not observe the law of your God and the law of the king, let judgment be executed upon him strictly, whether for death or for banishment or for confiscation of goods or for imprisonment" (7:11-26).[4]

Concluding Postscript

Verses 27-28 are again in Hebrew. Ezra adds his own personal postscript to this chapter: "Blessed be Yahweh the God of our fathers, who has put such a thing as this in the king's heart, to adorn the house of Yahweh which is in Jerusalem, and has extended lovingkindness to me before the king and his counselors and before all the king's mighty princes. Thus I was strengthened according to the *hand of Yahweh my God upon me*, and I gathered leading men from Israel to go up with me" (7:27-28, emphasis added).

Ezra's study of the Scriptures had expanded his world of reality. He could discern the hand of the Lord in the events of his life (cf. 7:6, 9, 28; 8:18; see also David's insights in Psalms 103 and 139). This awareness of God's overarching care of him only came as a result of prolonged meditation on the Scriptures.

We are all familiar with Joseph Gilmore's (1834-1918) hymn "He Leadeth Me." He describes in a poetic way the joy of knowing that the hand of the Lord is upon us (cf. Psalm 23:2).

---

4. Z. W. Falk, *Vetus Testamentum* 9 (1959), 88-89.

He leadeth me! O blessed thought! O words with heav'nly comfort fraught!
What'ere I do, where're I be, still 'tis God's hand that leadeth me.

This is not a privilege reserved for "super-saints," but can be experienced by all who sincerely desire to honor the Lord in their lives.

PART TWO

THE RETURN UNDER EZRA

EZRA 7:1--10:44

CHAPTER SEVEN

THE SECOND RETURN OF THE EXILES

EZRA 8:1-36

D. L. Moody, the great evangelist, once confided, "The world has yet to see what God can do with a man fully consecrated to him." Then he added, "By God's help, I aim to be that man." Ezra was a man wholly consecrated to the Lord, and these chapters record what God was able to do through him.

As we read through 7:1-28 we gain the impression that King Artaxerxes was a kind, benevolent sovereign, especially in his attitude toward Israel.[1] What is often overlooked is the fact that his attitude toward Israel was the result of his confidence in Ezra. Ezra, as we have seen, was a person of integrity, and Artaxerxes trusted him "permitting him to *visit* Jerusalem as Commissioner for Jewish Affairs."[2]

---

1. Cf. Plutarch, *Vita Artaxerxes*, c:1; and Diodorus Sicilus, *Works*, ix:71.
2. R. K. Harrison, "Artaxerxes," *International Standard Bible Encyclopedia*, Fully Revised by G. W. Bromiley et al, 4 vols. (Grand Rapids: Eerdmans, 1979), 1:306.

Ezra's amanuenses blended together Ezra's account with a record of events as they transpired. He began by giving us a copy of the letter Artaxerxes gave Ezra. Its opening statement is significant for it underscores the trust Artaxerxes had in him. "Now this is the copy of the decree which King Artaxerxes gave to *Ezra the priest, the scribe, learned in the words of the commandments of Yahweh and His statutes to Israel*: 'Artaxerxes, king of kings, to *Ezra the priest, the scribe of the law of the God of heaven*, perfect peace'" (7:11-12, emphasis added).

The reader can hardly overlook the accolades given Ezra. He was not the high priest, and did not rank high in the ecclesiastical echelon of those commissioned to safeguard the spiritual welfare of God's people.[3] His life, however, shows us that a person can have a powerful influence for good even if he is not numbered among the power brokers of his or her era.

Some critics have objected to the seemingly contrived contents of Artaxerxes' letter. Their protests center in the Jewish elements contained in it. They believe that the king would have been unfamiliar with these tenets. We note from Nehemiah 11:24, however, that Persian kings had advisors[4] who gave counsel in all matters relating to a spe-

---

3. When the people entered into a covenant (Nehemiah 9:38–10:8), the leading priests signed first. Ezra was not numbered among them. After that "the rest of the people, *the priests*, the Levites ..." signed the document. Ezra was probably in this second group.

cific subject people.[5] Once again the carping of the Bible's critics is shown to be devoid of substance.

Chapter 7:12-26 is again in Aramaic. Artaxerxes continued his dictation to the court recorder: "I issue a decree that all those of the people of Israel and the priests and Levites in my realm, who volunteer to go up to Jerusalem, may go with you. And whereas you are being sent by the king and his seven counselors[6] to inquire concerning Judah and Jerusalem, with regard to the Law of your God which is in your hand; and whereas you are to carry the silver and gold which the king and his counselors have freely offered to the God of Israel, whose dwelling is in Jerusalem; and whereas all the silver and gold that you may find in all the province of Babylon, along with the freewill offering of the people and the priests, are to be freely offered for the house of their God in Jerusalem--now therefore, be careful to buy with this money bulls, rams, and lambs, with their grain offerings and their drink offerings, and offer them on the altar of the house of your God in Jerusalem" (7:13-17).

The decree empowered Ezra (and those who wished to go with him) to take to Jerusalem the gifts given by the king and his seven counselors, along with the freewill offering of the people, and to insure that God's law was being observed. It further provided liberally for the sacrifices that

---

4. King Artaxerxes had a Jew named Pethahiah who was the king's representative in all matters concerning the people.
5. Cf. Williamson, *Ezra, Nehemiah*, 100.
6. Cf. Herodotus, *History*, 3:31, 71, 83-84; and Xenophon, *Anabasis*, 1:6:4-5.

were to be offered up in Jerusalem; commanded the treasurers in the provinces west of the Tigris-Euphrates River valley to provide whatever supplies Ezra might need; freed all Temple servants from taxation; and authorized Ezra to set up a judicial system that would extend to all Jews living beyond the borders of Judah.

Of interest is the fact that the king's decree mentioned "the Law of your God which is in your (Ezra's) hand." This implies that God's Word was in written form (and not oral tradition), and the king's words bear unwitting testimony to Ezra's work in collecting and propagating the sacred writings extant at that time.

Though Ezra was not appointed governor of Judah (as was Nehemiah a few years later), Artaxerxes gave him ample authority. He had come to appreciate Ezra's sagacity, and trusted him implicitly. Ezra's jurisdiction extended beyond those Jews who had remained in Palestine after the exile, to those living north of Samaria. All came under the same dual-law (i.e., the Law of the Lord and the laws of the Persians). And in administering these laws the Persian officials were to give Ezra all the support he needed.

In all probability recent hostilities in Jerusalem necessitated that the Temple be repaired, and to properly honor Yahweh it also needed to be embellished. Ezra praises God for His goodness in making all this possible. Further evidence of God's work on his behalf came when Ezra considered the Lord's work in the hearts of each of Artaxerxes' counselors who gave liberally of their own means to further the work of the Lord in Jerusalem. Such a realization strengthened him for the arduous task that lay ahead of him.

THE JOURNEY, 8:1-36

The Heads of Households, 8:1-14

We are not told of the difficulties Ezra faced as he informed the Jews living in Babylonia of Artaxerxes' decree. It would not be easy for them to relinquish their livelihood for a long journey and an uncertain future in Judah. The meeting place was the canal Ahava, possibly a tributary of the Euphrates near Babylon.

How many Jews might be expected to join him? Dr. Mervin Breneman took note of the emphasis on "family heads" (8:1), and wrote: "The emphasis on 'family heads' reminds us of the great responsibility of being the head of a family."[7] It is one of the tragedies of our times that fathers have relinquished their roles and no longer give proper leadership to their families.

Twelve "clans" are listed in these verses, and on twenty-four occasions Ezra uses the word "Israel." This would seem to imply that people from the northern tribes of Israel were among those who joined Ezra in the long journey to Judah.[8] If each family unit comprised a father,

---

7. Breneman, *Ezra, Nehemiah, Esther*, 138.

mother, and three children, those who gathered on the banks of the canal would total about 5000.

Of significance is verse 13. The entire family of Adonikam made the journey. None remained in Babylon. Their patriotism and religious zeal gave stability to their lives.

The Recruitment of Levites, 8:15-20

As Ezra looked over the people who began to assemble beside the Ahava, he did not find many Levites among them. We are left to conclude that the prosperity afforded them in Babylon did not compare favorably with the menial service assigned the Levites in the Law. Ezra, therefore, sent leaders to Casiphia to recruit men for the work of the Temple in Jerusalem. Those whom he chose for this task were capable men, skilled in acting wisely in difficult situations.

Thirty-eight Levites, with their wives and children, responded to Ezra's summons, together with the Nehinim (assistants to the Levites). In all, the group waiting by the waters of the Ahava was augmented by 220 men and their families.

The Spiritual Preparation for the Journey, 8:21-23

Though Ezra was aware of God's hand on him, he did not act presumptuously. He knew of the dangers they would face from robbers who preyed on travelers. He, therefore,

---

8. Cf. 2 Kings 17:1-6, noting esp. v. 6.

proclaimed a fast: "Then I proclaimed a fast there at the river of Ahava, that we might humble ourselves before our God to seek from Him a safe journey for us, our little ones, and all our possessions. For I was ashamed to request from the king troops and horsemen to protect us from the enemy on the way, because we had said to the king, 'The hand of our God is favorably disposed to all those who seek Him, but His power and His anger are against all those who forsake Him.' So we fasted and sought our God concerning this matter, and He listened to our entreaty."

In ancient Israel the whole nation was called upon to fast on the Day of Atonement (Leviticus 16:29, 32), but fasting was not a prominent part of their national life. During the exile it became more common (Zechariah 8:19), however, it was never intended to be an external rite (cf. Matthew 6:16-18; 23:14). When the Lord Jesus spent forty days in the desert in earnest prayer to the Father He was oblivious to His need of food. Only afterwards was He hungry (Matthew 4:2).

The Delegation of Responsibility, 8:24-30

But who would look after the gifts of the king, his counselors, and the people who had given willingly to those journeying to Jerusalem? Ezra wrote, "I set apart twelve of the leading priests, Sherebiah, Hashabiah, and with them ten of their brothers; and I weighed out to them the silver, the gold and the utensils, the offering for the house of our God which the king and his counselors and his princes and all Israel present there had offered. Thus I weighed into their hands 650 talents of silver, and silver utensils worth 100 talents, and 100 gold talents, and 20 gold bowls worth 1,000 darics, and two utensils of fine shiny bronze, precious as gold. Then I said to them, 'You are holy to Yahweh, and the utensils are holy; and the silver and the gold are a freewill offering to Yahweh, God of your fathers. 'Watch and keep them until you weigh them before the leading priests, the Levites and the heads of the fathers' households of Israel at Jerusalem, in the chambers of the house of Yahweh.' So the priests and the Levites accepted the weighed out silver and gold and the utensils, to bring them to Jerusalem to the house of our God."

The silver would have weighed approximated 780,000 ounces or 24.4 tons; the gold, about 120,000 ounces or 3.75 tons; and the darics (8:27) would have had a value of nearly 300 ounces of gold. Some scholars have estimated that this wealth would have provided the annual income of between 100,000 and 500,000 men.

Consecrated priests, with the help of some of the Levites, were commissioned to oversee the transportation of these gifts to Jerusalem (Numbers 3:6–4:33). Theirs was a sacred trust. Ezra's actions set an example for all who handle the gifts to the Lord. Though considered a mundane task by many in the church, it is a sacred duty.

The Journey, 8:31-32

"Then we departed from the river Ahava on the twelfth day of the first month, to go to Jerusalem. And the hand of our God was upon us, and He delivered us from the hand of the enemy and from ambush along the road. So we came to Jerusalem, and stayed there three days."

In 7:9 it states that Ezra and his company began their journey to Jerusalem on the first day of Nisan, whereas here we are told that they set out on the twelfth day of Nisan. Is this an example of an error in the Bible? No. The intervening period of time was spent recruiting the Levites.

Once again Ezra acknowledged the good hand of the Lord upon all who traveled to Jerusalem. They were protected from robbers who might easily have attacked so large a caravan. The presence of women and children, not to mention the allure of so much gold, would have made the caravan of returning exiles an inviting target.

The entire journey took about four months.

The Gifts Delivered, 8:33-34

On arriving in Jerusalem the repatriated Jews rested for three days. Then, "on the fourth day the silver and the gold and the utensils were weighed out in the house of our God into the hand of Meremoth the son of Uriah the priest, and with him was Eleazar the son of Phinehas; and with them were the Levites, Jozabad the son of Jeshua and Noadiah the son of Binnui. Everything was numbered and weighed, and all the weight was recorded at that time."

Meremoth was evidently the Temple treasurer who held an important position in the Temple hierarchy.

The exact weight of all the gifts may have been necessary so that Ezra could send King Artaxerxes signed certification that these gifts had been delivered. If this is so, then once again Ezra sets us an example how to handle the church's gifts and other assets so that all the activities of the church are above reproach.

A Grateful Conclusion, 8:35-36

"Then the exiles who had returned from captivity offered burnt offerings to the God of Israel: twelve bulls for *all Israel*, ninety-six rams, seventy-seven[9] lambs, twelve male goats for a sin offering, all as a burnt offering to Yahweh. Then they delivered the king's edicts to the king's satraps and to the governors in the provinces beyond the [Tigris-Euphrates] River, and they supported the people and the house of God" (emphasis added).

The first act of the returned exiles was to give expression of their thanks to God for His mercies. The sin offering took care of the uncleanness of the exiles. The burnt offerings signified the utter gratitude and praise of the repatriated Jews and their dedication to Him and His Laws.

Following these acts of thanksgiving and worship Ezra presented the documents investing him with specific authority.

---

9. The Apocryphal book of 1 Esdras 8:66 gives the number as 72. Cf. Fensham, *Ezra and Nehemiah*, 122.

As we conclude our survey of these chapters we cannot help but notice Ezra's continued reference to *the hand of Yahweh his God.... upon him.* How did he become conscious of God's special favor? We know from 7:6, 10, that Ezra had meditated on and ordered his life according to God's Word. As he did so he developed a special relationship with the Lord. This resulted in an expansion of his world of reality so that he could look beyond the temporal and see God's invisible hand of blessing resting on him.

A great man who left his mark on the Christian church was Dr. J. D. Jones. Those who came to hear him preach were impressed by the fact that (as one biographer has put it) his life was controlled by the message he preached. He was once asked for a definition of preaching. He replied, "It is a real man, speaking real things, out of real experience." And the genuineness of his walk with the Lord carried over into his care of others.

Ezra's experience of God's care of him should not be unique, for the Lord Jesus said that He would always be with His followers (note His words in John 14:20; 15:4; 17:21).

CHAPTER EIGHT

VALIANT FOR TRUTH

EZRA 9:1–10:44

In John Bunyan's *Pilgrim's Progress* he tells of a man named Valiant for Truth. Valiant had recently encountered three men who had tried to dissuade him from journeying toward the Celestial City. The first had invited him to become one of them. When he met with no success, the second turned on Valiant for Truth and told him to go back to the place from which he came. When he met with Valiant's bold assertion of his intent to continue to the Celestial City, the third man threatened that if Valiant did not accede to their desires he would die where he stood.[1]

Later on Valiant for Truth was met by a man whom Bunyan calls Great Heart. He inquired about his wounds. Valiant dismissed his injuries as minor and then claimed that his victory over his opponents had been achieved as a result of his use of the sword of the Spirit (i.e., the Word of God, cf. Ephesians 6:17; Hebrews 4:12).

---

1. *The Works of John Bunyan*, 3 vols., ed. by G. Offer (Carlisle, PA: Banner of Truth, 1991), I:232.

THE BROKEN LAW, 9:1-15

Ezra's Humility, 9:1-4

Ezra had been in Judah for about four months when the situation described in these verses was brought to his attention (cf. 7:9 and 10:9). His teaching of the Word of the Lord had begun to bear fruit among some of the people.[2] God intended Israel to be a holy race (lit. "seed"). They were not to mingle with the nations or adopt their customs (cf. Psalm 106:35).

When Ezra heard that many of the Jews had intermarried with people from the surrounding nations, he was devastated. He knew from Israel's history of the disastrous results that such a practice had brought upon the nation. The more he learned of these marriages the more alarmed he became. This practice had been going on for some time, and some of the culprits had already fathered children.

The New Testament shares a similar concern over intermarriage and commands believers not to intermarry with

---

2. This included passages such as Deuteronomy 7:1-6 (cf. Exodus 23:11-16) and Deuteronomy 23:3. See also Exodus 34:11-16 and Deuteronomy 20:10-18.

those who do not share their faith in the Lord Jesus (cf. 2 Corinthians 6:14-17).

So great was Ezra's grief and bewilderment that he tore his inner garment and outer robe, pulled out some of his hair from his head and beard, and sat down in stunned silence. Later, in recounting the events of this day, he wrote: "Then everyone who *trembled at the words of the God of Israel* on account of the unfaithfulness of the exiles gathered to me" (9:4). It is obvious that the people felt the need of godly leadership and guidance.

Too few Christians today "tremble" at the teaching of God's Word. Negative critics of the Bible have attacked its trustworthiness. As a result, people have lost confidence in the Scriptures. Passivity and a laissez-faire attitude now characterize many individuals and their churches. And this has resulted in an insensitivity to sin.

Through Ezra's teaching the Israelites in Judah had been newly awakened to the revealed will of God and the dangers of disobedience; and they treated what God had communicated through His Word with reverential awe.

Ezra's Confession, 9:5-15

The people continued to wait on Ezra until the time of the evening sacrifice (around 3:00 P.M.). It was then that Ezra turned his grief over God's broken Law into prayer. He knelt before the Lord. His prayer is amazing. It reveals his true humility, identification with God's people, and confession of sin (9:6-7a); God's righteousness in punishing

Israel's past sins (9:7b); His lovingkindness in relieving their bondage (9:8-9); Israel's present sins (9:10-14); and a doxology in recognition of God's righteousness (9:15).

Here is his prayer:

"O my God: I am too ashamed and humiliated to lift up my face to You, my God; for our iniquities have risen higher than our heads, and our guilt has grown up to the heavens. Since the days of our fathers to this day we have been very guilty, and for our iniquities we ... have been delivered into the hand of the kings of the lands, to the sword, to captivity, to plunder, and to humiliation, as it is this day" (9:6-7).

God had given clear instructions to the people through Moses and the prophets. His people were not to intermarry with the nations living in Canaan lest they learn their customs (cf. Deuteronomy 7:3-5; 23:3-4). God knew that the Israelites, as in the confrontation of Valiant for Truth, would be invited to join the ranks of those living in the land. If they refused, they would be told to go back to the land from which they came (i.e., Egypt). And if they did not do so, they could expect violent opposition from those who regarded them as interlopers.

In spite of the clear message from the Lord and the evidence of their past history, the people had disobeyed the Lord and the holy seed was in danger of being corrupted.

Ezra saw clearly the danger they were in. As Ezra continued his prayer, he said:

> "But now for a brief moment grace has been shown from Yahweh our God, to leave us an escaped remnant and to give us a *peg* in His holy place, that our God may enlighten our eyes and grant us a little reviving in our bondage. For we are slaves; yet in our bondage, our God has not forsaken us, but has extended lovingkindness to us in the sight of the kings of Persia, to give us reviving to raise up the house of our God, to restore its ruins, and to give us a wall in Judah and Jerusalem" (9:8-9).

Ezra was deeply conscious of God's mercy in restoring His people to the land He had promised to their forefathers. He also recognized that God had a special relationship with the people of Israel. He was their Suzerain, they were His vassals. This relationship gave Him the right to impose ethical demands on His people. His righteousness required that He punish His people when they violated His laws. Ezra also knew that the Lord is gracious and merciful; slow to anger and great in lovingkindness (Psalm 145:8).

Even though the Jews were still subject to the Persians, Ezra rejoiced in the fact that the Lord had given His people a new start.

> "But now, our God, what shall we say after this? For we have forsaken Your commandments, which You have commanded by Your servants the prophets, saying, '... do not give your daughters to their sons nor take their

daughters to your sons, and never seek their peace or their prosperity, that you may be strong and eat the good things of the land and leave it as an inheritance to your sons forever.' After all that has come upon us for our evil deeds and our great guilt, since You our God have requited us less than our iniquities deserve, and have given us an escaped remnant as this, shall we again break Your commandments and intermarry with the peoples who commit these abominations? Would You not be angry with us to the point of destruction, until there is no remnant nor any who escape? O Yahweh, God of Israel, You are righteous, for we have been left an escaped remnant, as it is this day; behold, we are before You in our guilt, for no one can stand before You because of this" (9:10-15).

We need to remind ourselves that though Ezra had recently returned to Jerusalem, the experience of the exiles was fresh in his mind. Now his hopes of establishing a godly theocracy had been dashed. It is no wonder that he bowed before the Lord in grief over Israel's sin. He realized that for a brief moment the Lord had graciously given them a tent "peg" by which they could secure their hope of future happiness. And He had done this even though the people of Judah were the vassals of Artaxerxes Longimanus. But Israel had shown its ingratitude and quickly returned to the sins of their fathers.

Though Ezra was not personally guilty of the sins of God's people, he identified himself with them. His prayer underscores the importance of taking God's commands seriously. In his confession of sin Ezra acknowledged God's mercy to His people, for He had not punished them as severely as their sins deserved. His anger was aroused when sin remained unconfessed. Ezra, therefore, threw himself and the people on God's mercy and pleaded that He not destroy His people.

In spite of the enormity of their sin, the Lord had punished them less than their sins deserved. What could be done to restore God's favor?

THE COVENANT, 10:1-44

As Ezra continued to pray and make confession, weeping and prostrating himself before the House of God, a large group of men, women and children gathered about him. They had been convicted of their sins, and their tears bore witness to their contrition. At last, a man named Shecaniah became spokesman for the group. He had not taken a foreign woman as his wife, but his father had done so, and he knew firsthand the evils of introducing paganism into the home.

He, too, identified himself with the sins of the people and then, speaking directly to Ezra, said: "But still there is hope. Now let us make a covenant before our God to send away all these women and their children, in accordance with the counsel of my lord [namely, Ezra] and of those who fear the commands of our God. Let it be done according to the

Law. Arise! This matter is your responsibility, but we shall be with you. Be courageous and act."[3]

Shecaniah realized that by taking foreign women into their homes they had broken God's law. He proposed that they correct their error by "sending away" their pagan wives. By returning to the homes of their parents these women could contract a new marriage.

Shecaniah called upon Ezra to take prompt action (10:4). His suggestion was based on the knowledge that Israel was to be a "holy seed," "a holy race" (9:2). Hope is to be found in Isaiah 6:13, where Israel is likened to "a stump [of a tree that] remains when it is felled. The holy seed is its stump." He may also have based his confidence on Deuteronomy 30:8-10.

And Ezra arose. Working with the priests and Levites and all Israel he made them take an oath to do as Shecaniah had recommended. This was followed by a proclamation sent throughout Judah summoning everyone to come to Jerusalem. Anyone who did not do so was to be punished (10:8).

On December 8, 457 B.C., all the men gathered before the House of God in Jerusalem. They were trembling in fear of what punishment might fall on them, and they shivered in the heavy downpour of rain.

---

3. W. R. Eichhorst, *Grace Journal* 10 (1969), 16-28.

Ezra called upon those who had taken foreign women into their homes to make confession to the Lord and do His will (10:10-11).[4] His proposal met with a heart affirmation (10:12). On account of the large number of people with foreign wives and the inclement weather, their leaders suggested that the people be allowed to return to their cities and then come back to Jerusalem at appointed times to have their specific case heard.

Four people opposed this proposal (10:15). Apparently they wished to keep their foreign wives. Meshullam was one of the four. Later, perhaps yielding to pressure from his brothers, he gave up his foreign wife (10:29). What happened to the other three is not told to us.

When the large number of Israelites began to present themselves before the elders, the priests were first (10:18-22). Seventeen had married women forbidden them by law. Among them were the sons of Jeshua who, with Zerubbabel, had been a part of the first group to return to Judah. They pledged to put away their foreign wives and sacrificed a ram as a guilt offering.

The next group were Levites (10:23-24). Theirs was a small group totaling ten persons in all.

They were followed by eighty-three or eighty-four lay Israelites. Some of these Israelites had children by these

---

4. W. C. Kaiser, Jr., *Hard Sayings of the Old Testament* (Downers Grove, IL: InterVarsity, 1988), 142-43.

foreign women, and it must have been very hard for the fathers to send away these children with their mothers.

Ezra, of course, believed in the sanctity of marriage. However, the moral dilemma he faced threatened the future of the nation.

The book of Ezra ends abruptly. Part of chapter 9 and all of chapter 10 were written by Ezra's secretary. After these events Ezra possibly returned to King Artaxerxes to give his report, leaving his secretary behind to look after affairs.[5] If this is what happened, it is easy for us to understand how the book would lack an appropriate ending.

Of particular interest is the part of Ezra's prayer in which he mentions a "remnant." The *Oxford American Dictionary*, edited by Eugene Ehrlich et al, defines a "remnant" as follows:

> **remnant** *n.* 1. a small remaining quantity or part or number of people or things. 2. a surviving trace of something. 3. a small piece of cloth left when the rest of the bolt has been used or sold.

The idea of a "remnant" when applied to the Jewish people finds a place in the writings of the Old Testament prophets (cf. Isaiah 10:5, 12, 20-21). God, speaking through His spokesmen, predicted that a remnant of Israelites, taken

---

5. We know that Ezra returned to Jerusalem during the administration of Nehemiah 8:1ff. and 12:1ff.

into captivity by the Assyrians and Babylonians, would be returned to the Promised Land. This promise was fulfilled when first Zerubbabel and then Ezra led Jews back to the Holy Land. This same thought was in Ezra's mind (9:8-15).

Isaiah also wrote of a yet future day when "the Lord will reach out His hand a second time to reclaim the remnant of His people" that would survive the Tribulation (Isaiah 11:11-12; see also Jeremiah 23:3-8; 31:7-8). After the Romans destroyed Jerusalem in A.D. 70, the Jewish people were scattered worldwide. Micah had predicted that the "remnant of Jacob" will intermingle with many peoples, but not be assimilated by them (Micah 5:7). Even though Israel was established as a nation in 1948, they have not yet been restored from all the nations of the world (Deuteronomy 30:2, 6; Jeremiah 31:33-37). These predictions still await fulfillment, and what Ezra accomplished in the fourth century B.C. will one day be effected on a much larger scale.

ESTHER

INTRODUCTION

Whenever I begin the process of researching and writing a new book, I am reminded of the wise words of Rudyard Kipling. He explained his approach in simple terms:

I keep six honest serving-men
   (They taught me all I knew);
Their names are What and Why and When
And How and Where and Who.
I send them over land and sea,
   I send them east and west;
But after they have worked for me,
   I give them all a rest.

This is a good procedure to follow, and I have read as widely as my limited library resources will allow.[1]

A careful reading of the Bible reveals that each book has a special purpose, and the Book of Esther illustrates very clearly God's providential care of His people. Lest we become intimidated by the word "providence," let us remind ourselves that it comes from the Latin *providentia* which means essentially "foresight" or "making provision beforehand." An essential component of providence is God's freedom to use different means to accomplish His ends.

The brief period of time covered by the Book of Esther (486 to 473 B.C.) describes events that come between the first and second parts of the Book of Ezra (i.e., between chapters 6 and 7). Looking back to the early chapters of Ezra, we find that patriotism on the part of the Jewish people had waned. They had settled comfortably into life in Babylon. This is evident from the fact that in 538 B.C., when Cyrus gave permission for any who wished to return to Judah, only 50,000 responded. The majority were content with the living they had made for themselves and their families in the land bordering the Euphrates River.

---

1. Of particular value are the following: A. T. Olmstead, *History of the Persian Empire* (1948); A. P. Stanley, *Lectures on the History of the Jewish Church*, 3 vols. (1879); George Rawlinson, *The Five Great Monarchies of the Ancient Eastern World*, 3 vols. (1897); Edwin J. Yamuchi, *Persia and the Bible* (1990); J. M. Cook, *The Persians* (1983); J. B. Bury, *History of Greece*, 3d ed. (1970); the histories of Diodorus of Sicily (also known as Diodorus Sicilus), Loeb Classical Library (1969), Herodotus, Loeb Classical Library, (1963), and Aeschylus, "The Persians," 2 vols., Loeb Classical Library (1963) Xenophon, *Cyropaedia*, 2 vols., Loeb Classical Library (1968); and the indispensable *Ancient Near Eastern Texts Relating to the Old Testament*, ed. J. B. Pritchard (1955).

Later, following Cyrus' death, Darius I Hystaspes became king of Persia (521-486 B.C.). He planned to add Greece to his empire, but when his forces attacked the Greeks they were defeated at the Battle of Marathon. Darius withdrew to Babylonia to plan another attack, but he died before he could implement his plans. His son, Xerxes (the Ahasuerus of the Book of Esther)[2] succeeded him (486-464 B.C.). It was during his reign that the events of the Book of Esther took place.

We shall have more to say about Xerxes as this study progresses. In addition to his plans to attack Greece, chapter 1 also introduces us to his queen, Vashti. Her name, which is spelled seven different ways in as many manuscripts, means "best" or "beloved" or "desired one." According to Herodotus her given name was Amestris.

As we read through this portion of God's Word we note God's providential protection of His people, the Jews. This has led a large number of scholars to conclude that the message of the Book of Esther is too limited, and that it has no place in the canon of Scripture. Dr. Alexander Raleigh in his *Book of Esther* has clearly and concisely refuted the

---

2. Xerxes' name is an attempt to transliterate into Greek the Persian *Khshayarsha*. The same word in unpointed Hebrew took the form '*Chshwrsh*, probably pronounced 'A*chshawarash*, but at a later time it was wrongly vocalized in early English Bibles as "Ahasuerus." For verification of this, see R. D. Wilson, *A Scientific Investigation of the Old Testament* (Chicago: Moody, 1959), 69, n.25.

sophistry of those who propound such theories.[3] Others object to Esther being included in the canon of Scripture because they believe it lacks spiritual value. These objections have been answered by Gleason J. Archer, Jr., in his *A Survey of Old Testament Introduction* (Chicago: Moody, 1994), 464-67, and Roland K. Harrison, *Introduction to the Old Testament* (Grand Rapids: Eerdmans, 1969), 1085-1102.

But a question naturally arises in our minds, "Who wrote the book?"

According to the *Babylonian Talmud* (Baba Bathra, 15a) the authorship of the book is attributed to the men of the Great Synagogue. Ezra was the founder of this group of scholarly teachers, and it is likely that he played a major role in drawing together the facts found in the history of Esther. Others believe that Mordecai wrote it, however 10:3 would militate against his authorship.[4] Other scholars have suggested different writers, but none of them is satisfactory. The Ezra and the men of the Great Synagogue seem to be the most likely source of this book.

If this is so, when was the book written?

Inasmuch as Xerxes' successor, Artaxerxes (464-424 B.C.) is not mentioned, the Book of Esther was probably written before he ascended the throne.

---

3. A. Raleigh, *The Book of Esther* (Minneapolis: Klock and Klock, 1980), 1-5.
4. Josephus, *Antiquities of the Jews*, XI:6:1.

The contents of the book may be divided as follows:

The Danger Faced by God's People, 1:1–3:15
The Decision Reached by God's Servant, 4:1–5:14
The Deliverance Gained by God's People, 6:1–10:3

The Book of Esther has many critics. The most frequently voiced objection is that God is not mentioned by name in any of its ten chapters. Though this may occasion initial surprise, it does not negate the book's theological significance. In reality, God is evident behind the scenes keeping watch over His own, for just when the Jews were about to be exterminated He orchestrated their deliverance. James Russell Lowell has eloquently expressed God's involvement in human affairs.

Once to every man and nation comes
    the moment to decide,
In the strife of Truth with Falsehood,
    for the good or evil side; . . .
Careless seems the great Avenger;
    history's pages but record
One death-grapple in the darkness
    'twixt old systems and the Word;
Truth forever on the scaffold,
    Wrong forever on the throne,--
Yet the scaffold sways the future, and,
    behind the dim unknown,
Standeth God within the shadow,
    keeping watch above His own.[5]

God exercises His providence in accordance with His sovereignty (Ephesians 1:11), His freedom (Psalm 115:3), and His character (Psalm 145:17-20; Acts 14:17; Romans 2:4; 8:28). The *Westminster Confession of Faith* states, "God, the great Creator of all things, doth uphold, direct, dispose, and govern all creatures, actions and things, from the greatest even to the least, by His most wise and holy providence" (cf. Hebrews 1:3; Colossians 1:17). The absence of all mention of God in this book only serves to emphasize the transcendent quality of His self-revelation.[6]

Not prepared to accept any answer to their querulous carping, these Bible critics refer to the Book of Esther as a "historical novel." But those who hold to this view are forced to confess that the writer was intimately acquainted with the administration of the Persian Empire, and especially the location and construction of the palace at Susa. Then there are those detractors who attack the Bible's historicity. For example, they allege that Mordecai, Esther's uncle, would have to be well over one hundred to have been deported to Babylon in 597 B.C. and still be alive and active

---

5. *The Complete Works of James Russell Lowell*, ed. H. C. Scudder (Cambridge: Houghton Mifflin, 1925), 67.

6. The Apocrypha contains "the Additions to the Book of Esther." These chapters were penned by some pious individual who wished to remove from the canonical book the stigma of apparent godlessness. Consequently we find in these chapters numerous prayers and references to God. The spurious nature of these chapters was early recognized by devout believers and the material was excluded from the Bible (Roman Catholic versions excepted).

in Babylon during the reign of Xerxes (cf. 2:6). In reality the relative pronoun "who" in 2:6 refers to Kish, Mordecai's great-grandfather.

And then there are those who claim that secular history knows nothing of Vashti, Esther, or Mordecai. We have already shown that Vashti was probably an affectionate name for Amestris, and a good deal is known of her,[7] so this objection vanishes into thin air.

Esther only became queen in 478 B.C. She reigned as queen during the period when Xerxes was more interested in his harem than in going to war,[8] and so there was little that would cause her name to be inscribed on tablets or find its way into the history books. However, without the information in this book we would not know of the origin of the Feast of Purim, and we would be left to speculate (as others have done) that it arose as a pagan myth. In reality, the Book of Esther gives adequate background to support the historicity of Feast of Purim, and *ipso facto* justifies our belief in the historicity of Esther.

As for Mordecai, Xerxes promoted him to the office of first minister, a position he held for at least eight years, and historic documents mention him by name numerous times.[9]

---

7. Herodotus, *The History of Herodotus*, IX:108-09.
8. G. Rawlinson, *The Five Great Monarchies of the Ancient Eastern World*, 3 vols., 2d ed. (London: J. Murray, 1871), III:470.

There is no reason, therefore, why we should doubt the historicity and accuracy of the Book of Esther.[10] Hers is a story of faithfulness and courage. And as we study this interesting book we will be amazed at the truths it contains.

---

9. A. Ungnad in the *Zeitschrift fur die alttestamentliche Wissenschaft,* LVII (1940-41), 240ff., and LIX (1942-43), 219. He cites evidence for a certain *Marduk-ai-a* as an official in Susa during the reign of Xerxes. Furthermore, the name *Mardukai* has also been found frequently in Late-Babylonian inscriptions. For further proof, see E. M. Yamuchi, *Vetus Testamentum* 42 (1992), 273.
10. See W. S. Watson's article on the authenticity and genuineness of the Book of Esther in the *Princeton Theological Review,* 1 (1903), 62-74.

PART ONE

THE DANGER FACING GOD'S PEOPLE

ESTHER 1:1–3:15

CHAPTER NINE

THE ROYAL BANQUET, 1:1-22

The year was 485 B.C. and Xerxes (Ahasuerus) had just ascended the throne of the Medo-Persian empire. He now ruled over many nations from the Indus River (modern Pakistan) to upper Sudan, and from the Aral Sea in the northeast to the Ionian Sea in the west.

Darius I, Xerxes' father, had attempted to add Greece to his extensive domain, but his army had suffered a crushing defeat at the Battle of Marathon and was forced to retreat. Darius set about building a new army and amassing all the materials needed for a fresh assault on Greece. Before he could accomplish any of his plans he died and was succeeded by Xerxes.

Display of the King's Riches, 1:1-4

Following his father's untimely death, Xerxes determined to erase the humiliation of Persia's defeat. He spent the first three years of his reign consolidating his position on the throne,[1] and then set about planning the defeat of the Greeks. To do this he began by inviting all the princes, army officers, nobles and officials from his 127 far-flung

---

1. Xerxes had to put down a rebellion in Egypt and an uprising in Babylon before he could begin to plan his campaign against the Greek mainland. Cf. Olmstead, *History of the Persian Empire*, 234-37.

provinces to come to Susa.[2] For six months in the year 482 B.C. he entertained these dignitaries, and during this time he impressed them with his vast wealth and shared with them his plans for adding Greece to his empire.

Description of the King's Banquet, 1:5-8

When the leaders of the people had been told of Xerxes' plan, and of the satrapies the bravest would receive, not to mention the riches they would bring home with them once they had defeated the Greeks, he gave a final banquet that lasted for seven days. It was held in the court of the garden of the king's palace.[3] The Bible recounts what took place:

"When these days were completed, the king gave a banquet lasting seven days for all the people who were present at the citadel in Susa, from the greatest to the least, in the court of the garden of the king's palace. There were hangings of fine white and violet linen held by cords of fine

---

2. The Persians had now assumed dominance over the Medes, and Xerxes had moved his base of operations from Persepolis to the citadel of Susa.
3. Cf. Rawlinson, *The History of Herodotus*, 357-64; Herodotus, *Histories*, Bk. VII. The biblical text seems to imply that the feast lasted for 180 days, but L. B. Patton in *Esther* (International Critical Commentary, [Edinburgh: Clark, 1908], 131) has offered the explanation that the writer, having first mentioned the banquet (1:3), explained Xerxes desire to impress his subjects with his wealth, before returning to his main topic (1:5).

purple linen on silver rings and marble columns, and couches of gold and silver on a mosaic pavement of porphyry, marble, mother-of-pearl and precious stones" (1:5-6).

Dr. A. L. Oppenheim has described the nature of these ornamental gardens. They were open structures in the form of a colonnaded hall that would allow for the free flow of any breeze during the hot summer.[4] The hangings that shaded the guests were of white and violet–the royal colors–and the contrasting colors of the marble columns, gold and silver couches, and the mosaic pavement of porphyry, marble, mother-of-pearl, and precious stones completed the king's ostentatious display.

Wine was drunk from golden horn-shaped vessels that were individually designed and beautifully decorated. Drinking was done according to the king's decree. No compulsion was laid upon any man.[5] Each person was free to imbibe as much of the royal wine as he wanted.

Description of the Queens Banquet, 1:9

Queen Vashti also hosted a feast for the women. It was held in the palace.[6]

---

4. A. L. Oppenheim, *Journal of Near Eastern Studies* 24 (1965), 330ff.
5. This was different from earlier times when guests were obliged to drink whenever the king did.
6. Herodotus, *The Histories*, Bk. V.

Herodotus refers to Xerxes' queen as Amestris, and this has caused some critics to conclude that the story of Esther is fictitious. However, as we observed in the Introduction, the name Vashti, which means "beloved" (or in our terminology, "sweetheart" or some other term of affection) and presumes that she had a given name. There is no reason to doubt that Vashti/Amestris were the same person.

Demand of the King, 1:10-12

Throughout the week of feasting, and as the wine loosened men's tongues, Xerxes' subjects probably spent time boasting of the greatness of their individual accomplishments and their prized possessions. Not to be outdone, Xerxes determined to show them his greatest treasure. We read:

> On the seventh day, when the heart of the king was merry with wine, he commanded Mehuman, Biztha, Harbona, Bigtha, Abagtha, Zethar and Carkas, the seven eunuchs who served in the presence of King Xerxes, to bring Queen Vashti before the king with her royal crown in order to display her beauty to the people and the princes, for she was beautiful (1:10-11).

But Queen Vashti refused to come at the king's command (1:12).[7]

The request was simple enough, what could possibly have caused such an adamant refusal?

Various explanations have been given: Vashti's jealousy over the attention Xerxes had given one of his concubines; the inappropriateness of having to leave her guests; Vashti's opposition to the proposed war with Greece; and her possible collaboration in a plot to murder Xerxes and take the throne. None of these are backed by suitable proof. And if all Xerxes required was her appearance, why not avoid any ill-feeling, put on her most beautiful royal gown, don a veil, place her crown on her head, and join her husband on the rostrum where he was reclining on a couch?

Obviously more was required of her.

Another solution to Vashti's refusal answers these problem. In a promiscuous society where women were valued for their beauty and sensuality, it was common for powerful and influential men to parade their wives and/or concubines naked in order to show off their beauty.[8] And though we find this thought offensive, the fact remains that such practices were commonplace at that time in history.

The drunken Xerxes obviously required Vashti to come before his guests naked. And this would have been reason enough for her to refuse, but J. Stafford Wright has argued convincingly that Vashti's refusal was on account of the fact

---

7. M. Breneman, *Ezra, Nehemiah, Esther*, Vol. 10, The New American Commentary (Nashville: Broadman &Holman, 1993), 307-08; Baldwin, *Esther*, 60-61; and J. G. McConville, *Ezra, Nehemiah, and Esther*, Daily Study Bible (Philadelphia: Westminster, 1985), 157-59.

8. Cf. Herodotus, *The Histories*, Bk.V.

that she was pregnant.[9] Ill-health during the early months of her pregnancy, compounded by the tiring task of supervising the servants during the 180 days when her husband entertained the leaders of his empire, would have been sufficient reason for her to spend as much time as possible in her private quarters. And if she was five-to-six months pregnant at the time of the seven-day banquet, as is likely, and had put on a reasonable amount of weight, not to mention being exhausted following the preparations for the feasting, then there is every reason for her to say, "Enough!"

But how could Xerxes have been unaware of his wife's condition? He obviously knew of her pregnancy, but he had been entertaining the officials of his empire for six months and Vashti's advanced pregnancy had in all probability escaped his notice[10] (cf. his neglect of Esther in 4:11*b*).

But imagine the gasp of surprise, followed by an uncomfortable silence, when Xerxes' eunuchs came and advised the king that Vashti had refused to come as ordered. Even today Vashti's impertinence has readers of the story arguing the issues of the need for a wife to be obedient to her less-than-perfect husband. And disagreements between a husband and wife should be discussed in private.

---

9. Vashti/Amestris was pregnant with Artaxerxes I. See J. S. Wright, "The Historicity of Esther," in *New Perspectives of the Old Testament*, ed. J. B. Payne (Waco: Word, 1970), 37-47.

10. In addition, the excessive amount of wine he had imbibed had dulled his thinking.

Decree of the King, 1:13-22

Vashti's refusal of Xerxes' request did not take into consideration the king's loss of face before the servants and all the important men of the empire! We are not surprised to read, therefore, that the king became furious. If we had been present, we might have seen his face become red and his body become contorted with rage. Then, choking back his anger and struggling to regain a modicum of dignity, he summoned the wise men who were well-instructed in the law and justice, and asked: "According to law, what is to be done with Queen Vashti, because she did not obey the command of the king delivered by the eunuchs?" (1:15).

This was a safe course of action for Xerxes to follow. The wise men of the realm, whom Xerxes consulted, formed an all–male judiciary. We do not know if they deliberated for any length of time, but their decision could have been predicted. Their spokesman, Memucan, replied:

> "Queen Vashti has wronged not only the king but also all the princes and all the peoples who are in all the provinces of King Xerxes. For the queen's conduct will become known to all the women causing them to look with contempt on their husbands by saying, 'King Xerxes commanded Queen Vashti to be brought into his presence, but she did not come.' This day the ladies of Persia and Media who have heard of the queen's conduct will speak in the same way to all the king's princes, and there will be plenty of contempt and anger. If it pleases the king, let a royal edict be issued by him and let it be written in the laws of Persia and Media so that it cannot

be repealed, that Vashti may no longer come into the presence of King Xerxes, and let the king give her royal position to another who is more worthy than she. When the king's edict which he will make is heard throughout all his kingdom, great as it is, then all women will give honor to their husbands, great and small" (1:17-18).

Memucan's counsel was shrewd, but it was anything but impartial. It was shrewd of him to include all men in the fallout of Vashti's conduct. He then recommended that Vashti (the title "Queen" no longer appears before her name!) never again be allowed to come into the king's presence. It did not mean that she was to be thrust out onto the streets to support herself as best she could, but that she be compelled to spend the rest of her days in the king's harem.[11]

As Joyce Baldwin has pointed out, "There is an appropriateness about her punishment. If she will not come when summoned, let her not come ever again."[12]

"This word pleased the king and the princes, and the king did as Memucan proposed. So Xerxes sent letters to all the king's provinces, to each province according to its script and to every people according to their language, that every man should be the master in his own house and the one who speaks in the language of his own people" (1:21-22).

---

11. Olmstead, *History of the Persian Empire*, 285.
12. Baldwin, *Esther*, 62.

But Memucan's counsel was flawed. As one of the wise men of Babylon he showed a remarkable lack of sound judgment. How could the law he proposed be implemented? Officers of the court could not enter every home throughout the 127 Provinces in order to observe the daily interaction of a husband and his wife; and if the courts allowed hearsay evidence it would be too easy for a husband to malign his wife in order to obtain a divorce.

Time for Reflection

As we summarize some of the lessons that lie latent in this chapter we find that Memucan stands out as one of those people who seem better skilled at getting others into trouble than in solving a problem in a just and righteous way. Such people have a unique way of ingratiating themselves into the confidence of their superior, but (as one friend of mine described them) they are like a big wheel with a flat tire; and they seldom make a meaningful contribution to their organization.

A second point has to do with Xerxes. At the beginning of the chapter he was the most powerful monarch of his day. At the end of the chapter, though still king, he is seen to be weak and indecisive, and easily led into making an unwise decision.

Third, we can see the hand of God in human affairs for the divorce of Vashti paved the way (as Memucan suggested) for the selection of another queen who would be better than Vashti; and in our next chapter we will be introduced to Esther.

CHAPTER TEN

THE ROYAL WEDDING, 2:1-18

The banquet of chapter 1 had ended disastrously. Vashti had been deposed, never again to see the king's face. The momentum that Xerxes had hoped for had fizzled like a damp firecracker. In spite of this setback, plans for war went ahead. Between 483-481 B.C. Xerxes was away from Susa, but the easy victory he had hoped for became a crushing defeat. The Greeks routed his army and demolished his navy. Feeling sullen and dispirited Xerxes boarded one of his remaining ships and returned to Susa. His anger toward Vashti had cooled, and he longed for her to come and comfort him.

The Proposal, 2:1-4

The opening words of 2:1, "After these things ..." do not specify how much later. Bible scholars, fast-forwarding to verse 16, realize that Esther did not become Xerxes' queen until the seventh year of his reign (i.e., 479 B.C.), or four years after the events of chapter 1, so Xerxes' depression must have lasted for some time.

The king's attendants noticed their sovereign's melancholy and preoccupation with concubines in his harem, and proposed that beautiful young virgins be sought for him. To accomplish this task they suggested that he "'...appoint overseers in all the provinces of his kingdom that they may gather every beautiful young virgin to the citadel of Susa, to the harem, into the custody of Hegai, the king's eunuch, who was in charge of the women; and let their cosmetics be given them. Then let the young lady who pleases the king be queen in place of Vashti.' The matter pleased the king, and he did accordingly" (2:3,4).

Herodotus[1] informs us that Xerxes should have taken a wife from the family of one of his seven counselors (some records mention only six). The suggestion that responsible men go to each of the 127 provinces and bring all the beautiful virgins to Susa would weaken the power of these counselors, for the suggestion of Xerxes' servants implied that the new queen would be a commoner. This proposal pleased Xerxes and he lost no time in giving the order for this proposal to be carried out.

The Choice, 2:5-15

We are now introduced to a Jewish family living in Susa. The head of the household is a man named Mordecai. His ancestor, Kish, had been brought to Babylon in 597 B.C. by Nebuchadnezzar, and the family had lived in Susa ever since.

Of course, there are those critics of the Bible who deny that a person such as Mordecai ever lived in Susa or served the king. His name, however, is similar to the Babylonian

---

1. Herodotus, *The Histories,* III:84. J. G. Baldwin, *Esther,* 71n, has observed that inasmuch as Xerxes was required to take a wife from one of the leading families "there was very good reason for silence on the subject of descent."

name Mardukaya, and there is a text dating from the last years of Darius I or the early years of Xerxes that mentions a Marduka who was a royal accountant on an inspection tour from Susa. Evidence points to Marduka and Mordecai being the same person.[2]

Mordecai had adopted his young cousin, Hadassah (meaning "myrtle"), for her parents had died leaving her an orphan. Because it was common for people to take a name indigenous to the country where they lived (cf. Daniel 1:6-7), Mordecai gave his cousin the name of Esther (meaning "star").

Whereas Vashti is spoken of as very attractive, Esther is described as "beautiful of form and face." The Bible implies that she was elegant and graceful, charming and refined, personable and possessed of those inner qualities that radiated outward and made all who met her glad for the encounter.[3] Beauty is a God-given gift, but it can also be a snare. In our day a beautiful girl is invariably the target of those individuals who view her as a "trophy" or a "conquest," and whose motives are less than honorable. Esther remained pure and chaste in spite of the pressures brought to bear on her. Her personality was carefully molded by her cousin Mordecai.

---

2. See C. A. Moore, *Biblical Archaeologist* (1975), 74.
3. D. J. A. Clines, *Ezra, Nehemiah, Esther,* New Century Bible Commentary (Grand Rapids: Eerdmans, 1984), 288, has drawn attention to the writer's repeated use of the word "pleasing" (2:4).

By now the reader realizes that Esther is the one who, in the providence of God, is to replace Vashti. But this was definitely not clear to Esther. All we are told is that when the king's "overseers" went throughout his empire, Esther was among those taken to the palace and given into the custody of a eunuch named Hegai, who was in charge of the women.

Esther was numbered among the 300 or 400 virgins from whom Xerxes would choose a successor to Vashti. When she was taken to the palace along with the others she "found favor" with Hegai.

Curiosity prompts us to ask, What special qualities did Esther have that set her apart from the others, causing Hegai to take a special interest in her? All the women were beautiful; all probably felt somewhat insecure, and all wanted to be chosen as Xerxes' new queen. Apart from her outward beauty, Esther was also mature and self-assured without being flighty or pushy. And she exhibited a practical wisdom that was evident in the respect she showed Hegai. It is no wonder that he favored her above the other virgins.

Mordecai had instructed Esther not to reveal her nationality, and her Persian name would lead people to conclude that she was a Persian who had been born in Susa. Of course, this raises the question, Why should she keep her nationality a secret? Was anti-Semitism widespread? A possible explanation may come from the fact that many of the Jews who had remained in Persia had become very wealthy. Their wealth had given rise to envy and jealousy. Rather than give occasion for any ill-feeling, Mordecai told

Esther to keep her identity a secret. But was this dishonest? No. If no one asked Esther of her nationality, she was not obliged to give it.

When Esther was taken into the harem, she began a twelve-month regimen of beauty treatments. As we have already noted, Esther "...pleased Hegai and won his favor. He immediately provided her with her cosmetics and special food. He also gave her seven maids selected from the king's palace and moved her and her maids into the best place in the harem" (2:9). The length of the beautifying process had another purpose: It was to insure that each candidate was not carrying someone else's child.

Bible students have wondered why Esther did not protest the food given her as Daniel had done (cf. Daniel 1:9). Her situation was different to his. If she were chosen to be Xerxes' queen, she would (if invited) dine with him. To complain about the food would create unnecessary tension and prove counterproductive. Being a woman of discretion, she cooperated with those who were responsible for her care (2:10).

Every day Mordecai walked back and forth in front of the court of the harem, and one of Esther's attendants would take him word of how she fared.

The year-long preparation of each young woman involved having ointments massaged into their skin to remove unwanted body hair, and oil of myrrh to cover any trace of body odor.[4] Then, one by one, as the young virgins who had completed their beautification went to spend the night with Xerxes they were told that they could take with them whatever jewelry and clothing they desired. In the evening they would be shown to the king's private quarters and in the morning they would be taken to the king's harem. They would not again "go to the king" unless he summoned them by name (2:13-14).

"Now when the turn of Esther ... came to go into the king's private quarters, she did not request anything except what Hegai, the king's eunuch who was in charge of the women, advised. And Esther found favor in the eyes of all who saw her.

"So Esther was taken to King Xerxes to his royal palace in the tenth month which is the month Tebeth [December/January], in the seventh year of his reign [479 B.C.]" (2:15-16).

The month Tebeth is in the middle of winter. It is cold and wet. The writer's mention of the month and year indicates that the search for a new queen had taken a long time.

The night Esther was shown into the king's private chambers she did not adorn herself with costly clothing and expensive jewelry. She contented herself with those things Hegai suggested. In this we glimpse her inner security. She did not feel the need to surround herself with things to enhance her sense of worth.

---

4. Cf. A. Brenner, *Journal for the Study of the Old Testament* 25 (1983), 75-81.

The Wedding, 2:16-18

Xerxes was so attracted to Esther that he stopped the contest. It was not her skill in lovemaking that won him over, for she had had no prior experience. Nor was it her outward beauty, though he was undoubtedly attracted to her because of her looks. He found her to be modest, personally confident, and was drawn to her quiet and gentle spirit. Esther possessed all of the qualities he was looking for in a queen, and he set the royal crown on her head.[5] This sudden decision on the part of the king to stop the contest reveals the extent to which Esther impressed him.

Since the choice of a new queen was one of great importance, Xerxes celebrated the occasion with a banquet (2:17-18). The holiday he proclaimed (lit. a "causing to rest") might have involved a remission of taxes, or a day's respite from work; and it was accompanied by the giving of gifts (probably food) "according to the king's bounty."

The King's Faithful Servant, 2:19-23

Our chapter concludes with a brief statement about the virgins who never spent a night with the king, and a brief statement about a plot to assassinate the king that Mordecai uncovered. We read that "When the virgins were assembled a second time, Mordecai was sitting at the king's gate." Drs. C. F. Keil and Robert Gordis are agreed that this gath-

---

5. Esther possessed the characteristics Xerxes lacked. Though he was unaware of the extent to which she complemented him, he nonetheless valued what he saw in her.

ering of the virgins must refer to those who never had the opportunity to compete in the contest to replace Vashti.[6] They went into the King's harem where they were subject to the same conditions as the other concubines.

Mordecai, who had already proved himself valuable to the king, had been made a magistrate or judge. He now sat in the king's gate, where he mediated disputes or adjudicated legal matters that did not require the attention of the high court officials. His new position also gave him access to the palace. How this is connected with the transfer of virgins from one part of the palace to the concubine's harem, is not told us. We do know that "...Bigthan and Teresh, two of the king's officials who guarded the door to his private quarters, became angry with Xerxes and sought to lay hands on him [to assassinate him]. But the plot became known to Mordecai and he told Queen Esther, and Esther informed the king in Mordecai's name. Now when the plot was investigated and found to be so, they were both hanged on a gallows; and it was written in the Book of the Chronicles in the king's presence" (2:21-23).

And so a very eventful year in Susa came to an end.

Time for Reflection

A commoner has seldom attained royalty. One upon whom royalty was bestowed was the late Grace Kelly

---

6. C. F. Keil, *Esther*, Commentary on the Old Testament (Grand Rapids: Eerdmans, 1980), 341, and R. Gordis, *Journal of Biblical Literature* 95 (1976), 47.

(1929-1982). Her stunning beauty placed her among the most attractive women in the world. Grace had been born into an Irish Catholic family in Philadelphia. She was schooled privately, before starring in several well-received movies. Grace's natural, unsullied beauty and thoughtful ways endeared her to all whom she met. In time she met Prince Rainier of Monaco and became his bride.

Royalty is not something to which we, in America, aspire. We are commoners, and even our exalted position in Christ seems too much for us to comprehend. But the Scriptures clearly state that as sons and daughters of God we will reign with Christ (cf. 2 Timothy 2:12; see also Revelation 20:4, 6; 22:5).[7] What happened to Esther, therefore, is an earthly illustration of what awaits us. As Matthew Henry pointed out, "Those who faithfully adhere to Christ and to His truths and ways, whatever it cost them, will certainly have the advantage of it in another world: If we be dead with Him, we shall live with Him (2 Timothy 2:11). Those who are called upon to suffer for Him on earth shall reign with Christ in heaven (2 Timothy 2:12)."

As we reflect on Esther chapter 2 we also see the providence of God unfolding in a way that enlarges our understanding of His control of people and events, when the normal channels of His self-disclosure (i.e., prophetic revelation or some inspired writing) are absent. He is sovereign,

---

7. M. Henry, *Commentary on the Whole Bible*, 6 vols. (Peabody, MA: Hendrickson, 1991), 6:676; see also R. L. Thomas, *Revelation 8-22: An Exegetical Commentary* (Chicago: Moody, 1995), 421-22.

even though Xerxes may sit on the throne. He gave Esther her beauty; He prompted Mordecai to adopt her; and He gave her favor (*hesed*, kindness) with Hegai.

Our sovereign Lord does not work the same way in every circumstance, but it is comforting for us to know that He "causes all things to work together for good to those who love Him, to those who are called according to His purpose" (Romans 8:28).

CHAPTER ELEVEN

THE ROYAL VIZIER, 3:1-15

Plots and would-be assassinations are common in the Near East. In light of this fact, we are not surprised to read that "After these things" (i.e., after the attempt on Xerxes' life planned by Bigthan and Teresh) he appointed a Vizier, or prime minister, to protect him and safeguard his interests. The man he chose for this exalted position was an Amalekite named Haman.

The Amalekites were descendants of Esau. Their history was summed up by Balaam, "Amalek was the first of the nations, but his end shall be destruction"[1] (Numbers 24:20). The Amalekites were a nomadic people and in Abraham's time lived southwest of the Dead Sea (Genesis 14:7). In the time of Moses they occupied all the desert of *et Tel* to the borders of Egypt, most of the Sinaitic peninsula, and southern Palestine. Although this people is prominent in the Old Testament, they were wanderers going wherever pasture and trade took them, and we are not surprised that archaeologists have not as yet uncovered anything concerning them.

The Amalekites were always bitter enemies of Israel. Sometimes they attacked Israeli villages alone, and sometimes they raided them in conjunction with other Bedouin

---

1. Edom did not survive the Babylonian experience, even though its people were not deported (Malachi 1:2-5).

tribes. Their first unprovoked attack on Israel was at a place called Rephidim while the recently emancipated slaves were leaving Egypt (1445 B.C.). Israel had no organized army and used farming implements as weapons. Moses instructed Joshua to assemble able-bodied men to repulse the attack. A fierce battle ensued. After Israel had won the victory, the Lord instructed Moses to write an official record of the engagement as a memorial (Exodus 17:14, 16). We are not surprised to read that from this time onward there was intense hostility between the Israelites and the Amalekites.

The New Overseer, 3:1-4

"After these events Xerxes (Ahasuerus) promoted Haman,[2] the son of Hammedatha the Agagite, and advanced him and established his authority over all the princes who were with him and all the king's servants who were at the king's gate bowed down and paid homage to Haman; for so the king had commanded concerning him. But Mordecai neither bowed down nor paid homage" (3:1-2).

Haman, writes Dr. Clarence Edward Macartney, "...is one of the most sharply etched characters in the Bible, and certainly one of the ugliest–monstrous in pride, hate, revenge, conspiracy, and appalling in his final fate and judgment. Yet there are things about Haman that can be studied with profit."[3]

---

2. See the character study of Haman by C. E. Macartney, *Chariots of Fire* (New York: Abingdon, 1951), 169-80.
3. Ibid., 170-71.

Why Xerxes promoted Haman to the second highest position in the empire is not told us. It is remotely possible that Haman was descended from the royal line of Amalek (i.e., an Agagite). He had evidently been in the service of Xerxes for several years, and he had become very rich. He was obviously loyal to the king, and so won his favor. Judging from his character we conclude that he is probably to be numbered among those who exploit and abuse those under them, so that they are hated and distrusted by their subordinates.

How do we know this? Why else would Xerxes *command* all who saw Haman to prostrate themselves before him.[4] The king obviously wanted everyone to give his new vizier the same kind of reverence they would give him or one of their gods. Mordecai, however, refused such obeisance. He apparently had both religious and political reasons for his refusal.[5]

---

4. The Hebrew word is *shachah*, "to prostrate oneself, show obeisance" implied lying down flat on the ground with the hands and feet extended. It is a word used in connection with a suppliant's relation to God (or a god). It differs from *yikra*, "to bow, to bend the knee" that is commonly used in the Old Testament in the sense of showing respect to superiors (2 Samuel 14:4; 18:28; 1 Kings 1:16).
5. Classical writers make reference to two provincial governors who sat near the palace entrance. Perhaps they were Haman and Mordecai. If so, then Mordecai would have known enough about Haman not to bow before him. See Herodotus, *The Histories*, III:120; and Xenophon, *Cyropaedia*, VIII:1:6.

The king's servants observed Mordecai's deliberate disrespect and asked him the reason. We read: "Then the king's servants who were at the king's gate said to Mordecai, 'Why are you transgressing the king's command?' Now it was when they had spoken daily to him and he would not listen to them, that they told Haman to see whether Mordecai's reason would stand; for he had told them that he was a Jew" (3:3-4).

The question addressed to Mordecai was a respectful one, given Mordecai's high standing in Xerxes' court. At first Mordecai did not answer them, but ultimately he told them he was a Jew and that the kind of obeisance that Xerxes required was reserved for God alone. This answer surprised the king's officials who awaited the king's bidding, for they did not have this kind of exalted view of their gods.

The New Danger, 3:4-6

Some of the king's servants, partly out of curiosity but mainly out of a desire to ingratiate themselves into the vizier's good graces, told him of Mordecai's actions. At first Haman had not noticed that Mordecai acted differently to the other officials, but when he was told that Mordecai was a Jew old religious hatreds were revived. He remembered that the sacred Scriptures of the Hebrews mentioned that Israel's king would be greater than Agag (the titular title of the kings of the Amalekites. Cf. Numbers 24:7), and he recalled stories told him in his youth about King Saul who had been instructed to exterminate his people (1 Samuel 15). Old hostilities were reborn, and he immediately began to think of ways in which he could kill all the Jews as Saul had once been instructed to wipe out his people.

Anger is an intense emotional reaction resulting from one or more of the following: rejection, frustration, or humiliation. It is sometimes expressed in overt behavior or it may be repressed. When repressed it becomes like a reservoir of sludge that wells up until it bursts its banks and gushes out. This is generally followed by a calming effect, but unless the cause(s) is treated in a wholesome way, the cycle will repeat itself. Though several Christian writers have written on the beneficial aspects of anger, it is most often destructive. When we consider the fruit of the Spirit (in contrast to the lust of the flesh) we find that self-control and love of others are the appropriate keys for controlling our aggressive impulses.

A New Strategy, 3:7-15

Haman wanted to be sure his plans would succeed and so, beginning in the first month, which is the month Nisan (i.e., March-April), in the twelfth year of King Xerxes reign (474 B.C.), he had Pur (that is the lot) cast before him from day to day and from month to month, until the twelfth month, that is the month Adar (February-March of the next year) in order to determine the most auspicious time for the extermination of the Jews. Casting lots shows us how superstitious he was, and the fact that he persevered with this practice for such a long time gives us a clear indiction of the depth of his hatred.

We, in our sophisticated culture, might conclude that Haman's method of determining the most propitious time for the destruction of the Jews was both primitive and pagan. We, however, often unwittingly indicate the extent to which ungodly practices have permeated our lives and culture by the superstitious way we seek for signs. Dr. Mervin Breneman has observed that "...many forms of a basically pagan worldview pervade our modern world and even [our] Western culture. Thus there is an increase in spiritism, horoscopes, magic, and various forms of Oriental religions that are based in pantheism. Some such as Transcendental Meditation and the New Age, are a subtle mixture designed to offer guidance that is misplaced and erroneous."[6]

Once the day for the destruction of the Jews had been determined, Haman sought the king's consent. His cunning is evident. He pretended to be motivated by a desire to secure the king's welfare. He said, "There is a certain people scattered and dispersed among the peoples in all the provinces of your kingdom; their laws are different from those of all other people and they do not observe the king's laws, so it is not in the king's interest to let them remain. If it is pleasing to the king, let it be decreed that they be destroyed, and I will pay ten thousand talents of silver into the hands of those who carry on the king's business, to put into the king's treasuries" (3:8-9).

---

6. Breneman, *Ezra, Nehemiah, Esther*, 329.

He dissuaded Xerxes from investigating the matter for himself by referring to the Jews as "a certain people scattered abroad and dispersed" among all the ethnic groups that made up the empire. He then went on to state that they have their own legal system and ignore the laws that maintain a quiet and peaceful government. This immediately branded them as rebels who were guilty of disloyalty to the crown. The next logical step was easy: They should be destroyed.[7]

Haman shows the extent to which he had anticipated all possible objections. The destruction of these people would reduce the king's revenue. Haman, therefore, proposed to make up the king's loss from his own wealth. Ten thousand talents of silver would amount to 12,000,000 ounces. (Of course, Haman intended to reimburse himself from the wealth confiscated from the Jews.)

Based upon Haman's information Xerxes concluded that the dissidents to be killed were distant aliens and hostile to his cause. To give Haman the necessary authority to carry out his plan, Xerxes "...took off his signet ring from his hand and gave it to Haman ... the enemy of the Jews" (3:10).

---

7. The destruction of an entire group of people was not unheard of. Herodotus, *The Histories*, III:64-80 records the massacre of the Magi. At this point one should consult a map of the Persian empire to ascertain how extensive the massacre would be (i.e., from the Aral Sea in the north to the Arabian Sea in the south; from India in the east to Thrace [bordering Macedonia] in the west, including all of modern Turkey as well as Egypt and Lybia).

Verse 11 seems to imply that Xerxes declined the money Haman had promised to place in his coffers. It seems more likely, based on precedent, that he was giving Haman permission to take the spoils of the Jews for himself.

We can imagine the alacrity with which Haman called the king's scribes and dictated to them the content of the letter that was to be sent out to each official. The biblical historian recorded what took place:

> Then the king's scribes were summoned on the thirteenth day of the first month, and it was written just as Haman commanded to the king's satraps, to the governors who were over each province and to the princes of each people, each province according to its script, each people according to its language, being written in the name of King Xerxes and sealed with the king's signet ring. Letters were sent by couriers to all the king's provinces to destroy, to kill and to annihilate all the Jews, both young and old, women and children, in one day, the thirteenth day of the twelfth month, which is the month Adar, and to seize their possessions as plunder. A copy of the edict to be issued as law in every province was published to all the peoples so that they should be ready for this day. The couriers went out impelled by the king's command while the decree was issued at the citadel in Susa; and while the king and Haman sat down to drink, the city of Susa was in confusion (3:12-15).

Ironically, the date of the pogrom was the day before the slaying of the Passover lamb (Exodus 12:6). That occasion celebrated God's deliverance of His people from Pharaoh's cruel oppression. Would the Lord intervene now to spare their lives?

The royal mail carried the king's despatches by courier via a "pony express" to the farthest bounds of the empire. The extermination of the Jews was made explicit by the words "destroy, slay, annihilate," and the decree extended to everyone: young and old, men, women and children.

The decree was to be proclaimed giving people adequate time so that suitable preparations could be made.

The last part of verse 15 is very revealing. Xerxes was pleased with the way in which his new vizier had handled his affairs. Haman was evidently pleased, for the issue that had gnawed at him for so long was soon to be resolved. But while the collaborators celebrated with a suitable supply of the royal wine, the city of Susa is perplexed over the cause for such a Draconian[8] decree.

Time for Reflection

First, as we review this material we are reminded of God's promise to Abraham, "I will bless you, and make your name great; and so you shall be a blessing; and I will bless those who bless you, and the one who curses you I will curse" (Genesis 12:2-3). Haman and all those who seek to do the Jews harm should pay careful attention to this promise (cf. Isaiah 54:17).

---

8. Named after Draco, a Greek, who established harsh and inflexible laws in ancient Athens.

Second, Haman's anger turned to hate when he found out that Mordecai was a Jew. To our knowledge Jews had never done him any harm, but he ruminated on the history of his people and determined to blot out all Jews in all lands under Xerxes' power. It is significant that people tend to hate the opposite of what they love and to love the opposite of what they hate (Micah 3:2f.; Matthew 5:43-44; cf. Psalm 109:5). The ease with which hate can become a part of one's personality underscores the importance of the Apostle Paul's admonition not to let the sun go down on our wrath (Ephesians 4:26).

Third, Haman cast lots as a way of obtaining guidance from the gods. It is true that before the coming of the Holy Spirit Jews cast lots to determine the will of God (Proverbs 16:33; 1 Chronicles 25:8). The Lord Jesus told His disciples that it was necessary for Him to go away, but that He would send the Holy Spirit to them, and He would guide them into all truth (John 16:13). Since the giving of the Holy Spirit to indwell all believers, we receive guidance as He illumines the Word (Psalm 119:9, 11, 59, 105, 130, 133); enables us to pray (Psalm 25:4-5; James 1:5-6); helps us to exercise wise discernment (Proverbs 6:20-22; Acts 15:28); and leads us through a mature discernment of the issues (Psalm 1; Proverbs 11:3).

PART TWO

THE DECISION REACHED BY GOD'S SERVANT

ESTHER 4:1–5:14

CHAPTER TWELVE

THE QUEEN'S INTERVENTION

ESTHER 4:1–5:14

Some years ago my wife and I visited Greece. Across the street from our hotel was the remains of the Temple of the Olympian Zeus. After breakfast we walked across the street and strolled among the ruins. I stood next to one column that had fallen down and my wife took a picture. This colossal pillar, broken into sections, had a diameter almost as thick as I am tall. As I stood there, I was reminded of the words of Seneca, "Anger is like those ruins which break themselves upon what they fall."[1]

The truth of this statement will be borne out in Haman's life.

Reaction of the Jews, 4:1-14

Chapter 3 closed with Xerxes (Ahasuerus) and Haman sitting down to drink wine while people in the city of Susa were confused by the contents of the letter Haman had written in the king's name. Mordecai was doubtless among the first to hear of the edict to murder all the Jews, and as a sign of his intense grief he tore his clothes, dressed in sackcloth

---

1. Seneca, *De Ira*, Bk. *I*, sec.1.

and put ashes on his head. Sackcloth (made out of goat hair) was the official apparel of a mourner. A Greek manuscript of on the Book of Esther says that "he (Mordecai) uttered these words aloud: *Airetai ethnos meden edikekos,* 'A people are going to be destroyed, who have done no evil!'"

His first instinct was to acquaint Queen Esther with the news (4:2). This law is not mentioned elsewhere in the writings of the Persians that have come down to us, but its principle that nothing of an evil omen is to be obtruded on the monarch has been recognized throughout the East in all ages.

The celebrated Near Eastern scholar, Dr. Cyrus H. Gordon, has drawn attention to a distinctively Iranian institution which survives to modern times. It is known as *kitman*, and may be translated "dissimulation." According to this custom an individual is permitted to deny his or her religion and pose as a member of another faith if confronted with acute personal danger. According to Professor Gordon Iranian Shiites are permitted to pose as Sunnites when going on a pilgrimage to Mecca.[2] It is possible that the Jews in the Persian empire did not avail themselves of this provision, for to do so would be to turn their backs on the traditions of their people. We are surprised, however, that this decree did not drive them to pray to God for deliverance!

When Esther became aware of Mordecai's situation she sent clothes to him so that he might enter the palace. Mor-

---

2. C. H. Gordon, *Riddles in History* (New York: Crown, 1974), 88-89.

decai, however, refused to accept them. Esther's second attempt to find out the reason for Mordecai's behavior was to send Hathach to learn the reason for his grief.

"Mordecai told him all that had happened to him, and the exact amount of money that Haman had promised to pay to the king's treasuries for the destruction of the Jews. He also gave him a copy of the text of the edict which had been issued in Susa for their destruction, that he might show it to Esther and inform her, and to order her to go in to the king to implore his favor and to plead with him for her people" (4:7-8).

Hathach had been appointed by Xerxes to wait upon Esther, partly (as is still the case in the East), to serve her, and partly to observe her conduct and report back anything of an untoward nature. Oriental despots are never exempt from fears of jealousy and suspicion.

Mordecai's language in his communique to the Queen was exceedingly strong. We would like to think that he was imploring her to act on behalf of her people, and not commanding her. What he now asks her to do will necessitate that she make known her Jewish roots.

This was a difficult assignment that was made all the more difficult by the fact that Xerxes had not invited her to share his bed for thirty days. Though Xerxes delighted in Esther he was personally weak and insecure, and there were times when he preferred the frivolous company of his concubines to the stabilizing power of his wife. As a result he tended to neglect Esther.[3]

Esther faced danger if she approached the king uninvited. The Persian kings surrounded themselves with an almost impassable set of regulations. As far as I can ascertain the law alluded to in verses 9-11 was first enacted by Deioces, king of Media, and afterward, when the empires of Media and Persia were united, it was adopted by the Persians. All business had to be transacted and petitions submitted to the king through his ministers. Although this restriction was not intended to apply to the queen, yet from the strict and inflexible character of the Persian laws, and the extreme desire to exalt the majesty of the sovereign, even his favorite wife was not exempt.

Resolve of the Queen, 4:15-17

We would have thought that the crisis precipitated by Haman's decree would have given the Jews an excellent opportunity to entreat God's favor and pray for deliverance. If any prayers were uttered, the Bible is silent about them. Instead Esther determined that she and her maids, Mordecai and all the Jews in Susa, should fast before she went to see the king.

The "three days, night and day" (4:15) do not imply a total of 72 hours. In Hebrew thought a part of a day was counted as a whole day, and this explains how the fast could extend for "three days, night and day," and yet end on the third day (5:1).

---

3. See C. J. Barber, *You Can Have a Happy Marriage* (Nashville: Nelson, 1988), 113.

Esther's bold statement, "and if I perish, I perish" (4:16) reveals her courage that backed up her resolve.

Invitation to a Banquet, 5:1-8

On the third day Esther put on her royal robes and stood in the inner court of the palace, in front of the king's hall. The king was sitting on his royal throne in the hall, facing the entrance. When he saw Queen Esther standing in the court, he was pleased with her and held out to her the gold scepter that was in his hand. So Esther approached and touched the tip of the scepter (5:2).

Then the king asked, "What is it, Queen Esther? What is your request? Even up to half the kingdom, it will be given you." To this, Esther replied, "If it pleases the king, let the king, together with Haman, come today to a banquet I have prepared for him."

It was not only natural, but, on such occasions, highly proper for the queen to put on her royal robes. These must have been very beautiful and enhanced her natural beauty.[4] After not having seen Esther for thirty days, Xerxes had perhaps forgotten how beautiful she was. And seeing her, his curiosity was aroused. Why had she come to him?

When Esther approached Xerxes he was sitting on his royal throne with his golden scepter in his hand. His seat was not a throne according to our ideas of one but simply a

---

4. Of course, the king's attire had to be even more glittering. Cf. Olmstead, *History of the Persian Empire*, 109-11.

chair, and so high that it required a footstool. It was inlaid with gold, and covered with a splendid tapestry. No one, under pain of death, might sit on it.

Xerxes held out to Esther the golden scepter that was in his hand (5:2).

The golden scepter is illustrated in sculptures on monuments in both Persia and Assyria. In the bas-reliefs of Persepolis we see king Darius enthroned in the midst of his court, and walking abroad in regal state; in either case he carries in his right hand a slender rod or wand, about equal in length to his own height, ornamented with a small knob at the summit. In the Assyrian alabasters, as well those found at Nimrod and Khorsabad, "the great king" is furnished with the same mark of royalty–viz., a slender rod, but one destitute of any knob or ornament. On the Khorsabad reliefs the rod is painted red, doubtless to represent gold; proving that "the golden scepter" was of precious metal. It was commonly held in the right hand, with one end resting on the ground, and that whether the king was sitting or walking.

Xerxes extended his scepter to Esther as a token that not only her intrusion was pardoned, but that her visit was welcome. He then went on to promise her a favorable response to any petition she might make. "It shall be even given you to the half of the kingdom" was a cliche that originated in the Persian court and denoted great liberality (cf. Mark 6:23).

Esther seems to have been afraid to make her real request of Xerxes too abruptly, and wanted to do it when she could also accuse Haman of genocide. Her response, therefore, was tactful: "If it pleases the king, may the king and Haman come this day to the banquet that I have prepared for him" (5:4).

The suggestion pleased the king and he immediately sent for Haman so that they might do as Queen Esther had requested.

After the main course had been enjoyed, it was customary in Persia for guests to continue the banquet for a considerable time with fruits and wine. During this part of the feast Xerxes again asked Esther "What is your petition, for it shall be granted to you" (5:6).

Esther saw that she was gaining on the king's affections; but she was not yet sufficiently assured how to proceed. Desiring to further ingratiate herself into the king's favor, she asked Xerxes and Haman to come to a second banquet the next day. And the offer was accepted.

The question is often asked, "Why did Esther make the king wait?" It is true that delay adds suspense, but in quick tempered people this is risky. Xerxes mood may have changed, particularly if he felt that Esther was trying to manipulate him. On the other hand, Esther probably sensed that the time was not right for her to make her request, and so asked Xerxes and Haman to come to another banquet the following day. Dr. Charles C.. Ryrie has observed, "It was providential that Esther apparently lost her courage to expose Haman before the king at the first banquet and so held a second one the next day. During the intervening night, the events of chapter 6 took place, making it much easier for Esther to expose Haman at the second banquet."[5]

When Pride Precedes a Fall, 5:9-14

Haman's happiness depended on circumstances. When he left the palace after having been so significantly honored, and saw that Mordecai did not bow before him, his euphoria evaporated. With all that he had in riches and power, the one "fly" in his jar of "ointment" (Ecclesiastes 10:1) made him dissatisfied.

If Mordecai was not impressed with Haman's sudden rise to power, Haman knew of others before whom he could recount his greatness. Calling together his friends and his wife "...Haman recounted to them the glory of his riches, and the number of his sons, and every instance where the king had magnified him, and how he had promoted him above the princes and servants of the king." He then went on to tell them that, "Even Esther the queen let no one but me come with the king to the banquet which she had prepared; and tomorrow also I am invited by her to dine with the king." Then his mood changed, "Yet all of this does not satisfy me every time I see Mordecai the Jew sitting at the king's gate" (5:11-13).

---

5. Ryrie Study Bible, Expanded Edition (1995), 770. And, as J. G. McConville has pointed out, the delay allowed time for Haman's misguided self-confidence to mature (Ezra, Nehemiah, Esther, 177).

Pride will always cause its possessor to be unhappy. Haman had such a high opinion of his own worth, that he conceived himself defrauded by every one who did not pay him all the respect and homage which he believed to be his due.

Haman's wife and friends seem to have been cast in the same mold as Haman. Without any thought of the hurt it would inflict on Mordecai's family, they suggest that he "Have a gallows fifty cubits (75 feet) high made and in the morning ask the king to have Mordecai hanged on it." And after this go joyfully with the king to the banquet (5:14). Their advice pleased Haman, so he had the gallows made.

The gallows–probably a pole sharpened on one end on which a person was impaled– was an excessive height, almost as high as the city walls. This ostentatious act was designed to show all who saw it how great was Haman's power (5:14).

Time for Reflection

As we reflect on these chapters, we notice how in 4:1-3 Mordecai illustrates for us the importance of being maturely in touch with one's emotions. Tearing one's clothes and going about in sackcloth and ashes was widely practiced in Old Testament times (e.g., Genesis 37:34; 2 Samuel 1:11; Isaiah 3:24; Daniel 9:3; etc.). According to Herodotus the Persians of Xerxes' time tore their clothes to show their grief when their fellow-countrymen were defeated at Salamis.[6]

Our grief needs to be handled maturely if we are to avoid its effects on our emotions and physical well-being.

Second, Mordecai's words addressed to Esther, "who knows but that you have come to royal position for such a time as this?" hint at his belief in God's providence in placing Esther on the throne for the specific purpose of saving her people from annihilation (4:14). And Esther's response, "if I perish, I perish" (4:16) places her in the company of other brave women who have taken their lives in their hands in time of great danger.

We cannot always live comfortable, secure lives. There comes a time when each of us must take a stand for what we believe.

Third, as we shall see, Haman's rabid hatred of the Jews (and of Mordecai in particular) will pave the way for his downfall. He had every outward benefit to make him happy, but instead he nursed his wrath to keep it warm. He failed to realize that the soul was made for God, and nothing but God could fill it and make it happy. Angels in glory could not be happy when they sided with Satan and cast off their allegiance to their Maker. Solomon, in all his glory, possessed everything his heart could desire, but found it to be vanity and vexation of spirit. Haman's soul needed God as its center in order to be happy. And he, though the prime

---

6. Herodotus, *The Histories*, VIII:99. In our Western culture we are not demonstrative when it comes to expressing our grief. How to do this in an appropriate manner has been described in *Through the Valley of Tears* (Wipf and Stock, 2000).

favorite of the king, was wretched because Mordecai did not bow before him.

All of this reminds us of the Apostle Paul's teaching on contentment: "Therefore I am well content with weaknesses, with insults, with distresses, with persecutions, with difficulties, *for Christ's sake*; for when I am weak, then I am strong" (2 Corinthians 12:10, emphasis added).

CHAPTER THIRTEEN

THE UNRAVELING OF HAMAN'S PLAN

ESTHER 6:1–7:10

William Cowper penned a hymn that appropriately describes God's providence:

> God moves in a mysterious way His wonders to perform;
> He plants His footsteps in the sea and rides upon the storm.
> You fearful saints, fresh courage take: The clouds you so much dread
> are big with mercy, and shall break in blessings on your head.
> Judge not the Lord by feeble sense, but trust Him for His grace;
> Behind a frowning providence faith sees a smiling face.
> Blind unbelief is sure to err and scan His work in vain;
> God is His own interpreter, and He will make it plain.

THE REWARD OF THE RIGHTEOUS, 6:1-14

As we ponder the events described in this chapter, we gain a new understanding of God's providence. In the providence of God that which is expected to happen does not, and that which is unexpected does. The king had a sleepless night, and as a result the lives of Mordecai and Haman were changed dramatically. Whereas Haman was expecting to vanquish Mordecai whom he regarded as his enemy, it was Mordecai who was publically honored by Haman.[1]

---

1. Cf. Breneman, *Ezra, Nehemiah, Esther*, 343,

The Royal Insomnia, 6:1-3

The writer begins with the king's insomnia. His style is dramatic: "That night the king could not sleep." To try and induce sleep, Xerxes (Ahasuerus) ordered that a book chronicling the events of his reign be brought in and read to him.[2] The night dragged on. As morning dawned, the reader of these annals came to a section that described a plot against the king's life. This plot, as we know, was thwarted by Mordecai.

"What honor and recognition has Mordecai received for this?" Xerxes asked.[3]

"None," was the reply.

Joyce Baldwin has pointed out that for Xerxes to fail to honor a person who had saved his life was to be guilty of a serious omission that clearly needed to be rectified. Because of the delay in rewarding Mordecai, some specially noteworthy reward needed to be devised. Failure to do so now would cause the king to lose his reputation for just dealing.[4]

---

2. See Josephus' comments in his *Antiquities of the Jews*, XI, vi, 10.
3. Herodotus, *The Histories*, III:138, 140; VIII:85; IX:107, provides examples of such rewards.
4. Baldwin, *Esther*, 89.

The Royal Reward, 6:4-14

Xerxes wanted to remedy his oversight, and asked, "Who is in the court?" We read:

Now Haman had just entered the outer court of the palace to speak to the king about hanging Mordecai on the gallows he had erected for him. Xerxes' attendants answered, "Haman is standing in the court." "Bring him in," the king commanded.

When Haman entered, the king asked him, "What should be done for the man the king delights to honor?" Now Haman thought to himself, "Who is there that the king would want to honor more than me?" So he answered, "Let the man whom the king delights to honor be dressed in a royal robe the king has worn and ride on a horse the king has ridden--one with a royal crest placed on its head. Then let the robe and horse be entrusted to one of the king's most noble princes, and let him lead the one whom the king delights to honor through the city streets, proclaiming before him, "This is what is done for the man the king delights to honor!"

"Go at once," the king commanded Haman. "Get the robe and the horse and do just as you have suggested for Mordecai the Jew, who sits at the king's gate. Do not neglect anything you have recommended."

So Haman got the robe and the horse, robed Mordecai, and led him on horseback through the city streets, proclaiming before him, "This is what is done for the man the king delights to honor!" (6:4-14).

All the details build toward the climax of chapter 7. Even Haman's early arrival at court fits the point the biblical writer is making. In the providence of God the one who had planned the extermination of His people is paving the way for his own destruction.

Haman did not have an opportunity to place before Xerxes his request for the execution (i.e., the judicial murder) of Mordecai.[5] Instead, in response to the king's question, "What should be done for the man whom the king delights to honor?" he is betrayed by his own pride and arrogance. His illusions of grandeur cause him to think, "Whom would the king desire to honor more than me?" Imagine his humiliation and chagrin when he is made to honor the person whom he wishes to destroy. Truly "pride goes before destruction, and a haughty spirit before a fall" (Proverbs 16:18).[6]

Haman's humiliation was profound. He was forced to publically honor his enemy, and the people who lined the street to see what was happening could not help but take note of the sudden reversal of Haman's fortunes. Mordecai, however, was unaffected by the unexpected honor. After being paraded through the streets on the king's horse, he returned to his place at the king's gate. Haman, however, went home with his head covered as a sign of his mortification.

---

5. Moore, *Esther*, 67, describes the dramatic reversal of Haman's expectations.
6. This scene provides a good example of irony in the Bible.

Though Mordecai's reward had been long delayed, it came at a most opportune time.

Similarly, believers in Christ who have served the Lord faithfully may be tempted to ask, "Where is my reward? I've honored Him in all I have done. Now, as I look back on my life it seems as if I have toiled in vain, and spent my strength for nothing." The Lord Jesus, however, encouraged His followers to persevere through afflictions and false accusations. "Rejoice," He said, "and be glad, for your reward in heaven will be great (Matthew 5:11-12). And His final promise to His servant John was, "Behold, I am coming quickly, and My reward is with Me, to render to every man according to what he has done" (Revelation 22:12).

The psalmist pointed out, "Surely there is a reward for the righteous; surely there is a God who judges on earth!" (Psalm 58:11), and Mordecai shows that though a reward may be long delayed it will come in God's perfect time.

THE RECOMPENSE OF THE WICKED, 7:1-10

As we continue with events as they transpire in Haman's home, we note that the pace of the narrative is moving rapidly toward a climax. Haman's wife and friends gather around him to offer their advice, for Haman recounted to them everything that had happened to him. Then his friends, who have suddenly been cast in the role of "wise men," together with Zeresh his wife, predict the obvious, "If Mordecai, before whom you have begun to fall, is of Jewish origin, you will not overcome him, but will surely fall before him" (6:13b).

"While they are still talking with him, the king's eunuchs arrived and hastily brought Haman to the banquet which Esther had prepared" (6:14). The impression created by the biblical writer is that Haman is no longer in control of events.

The Queen's Request, 7:1-7

"So the king and Haman went to dine with Queen Esther," and when the banquet was over and while "they were drinking wine, the king again asked, 'Queen Esther, what is your petition? It will be given you. What is your request? Even up to half the kingdom, it will be granted'" (7:1-2).

Xerxes presumed that Esther would ask for material possessions, and he was totally unprepared for her plea: "My life ... my people." Her words were clear and concise. She continued: "We are sold, I and my people, to be destroyed by the cruel and perfidious scheme of that man who offered an immense sum of money to purchase our extermination." (Included in her petition were the exact words embodied in Haman's decree: "To be destroyed, to be slain, and to be annihilated.")

Xerxes was first stunned and then enraged as he contemplated the atrocity embodied in the expressions used in the decree. For her part Esther had awakened in the king the kind of emotions that could lead to prompt action.

But who had presumed to carry out such a plot?

Up to this point the queen has been careful to avoid all mention of Haman, but when the king asked, "Who is he, and where is he, who would presume to do this?" Esther was ready with her answer: "A foe and an enemy is this wicked Haman."

At this, Haman became terrified. He had not calculated on Xerxes' favorite wife being a Jew.

Quite naturally, Xerxes was furious. He had been used as a pawn and tricked into making a decree that includes the death of his beloved queen. Trying to keep his rage under control, he rose from off his couch and went into the palace garden. Clearly Haman was a traitor, and he must be dealt with accordingly. But how?

An Enemy Hanged, 7:8-10

While Xerxes was in the garden, Haman stayed in the banquet room to beg for his life. He saw that harm had been determined against him by the king. He fell on Esther's couch to plead for his life. When the king returned from the palace garden, he saw Haman on the couch where Esther was reclining. This was a total breach of palace protocol! Xerxes exclaimed, "Will he even assault the queen with me in the house?" As he spoke his servants covered Haman's face. The thought behind the covering of the face is that a criminal is unworthy any longer to look on the face of the one who has condemned him, and with his face covered he cannot plead for his life.

"Then Harbonah, one of the eunuchs who was before the king said, 'Behold indeed, the gallows standing at Haman's house fifty cubits high, which Haman made for Mordecai who spoke good on behalf of the king!' And the king said, 'Hang him on it.' So they hanged Haman on the gallows which he had prepared for Mordecai, and the king's anger subsided" (7:9-10).

The evil Haman had planned for Mordecai became his own punishment. It was an illustration of retribution in kind.

Many years earlier Solomon had written, "The righteousness of the upright will deliver them, but the treacherous will be caught by their own greed. When a wicked man dies, his expectation will perish ... The righteous is delivered from trouble, but the wicked takes his place" (Proverbs 11:6-8). How prophetic!

Those who lift up their hand against the Jews do so to their peril. God has entered into a covenant with them (Genesis 12:1-3). Consider His words in Jeremiah 31:35-37, "Thus says Yahweh, who gives the sun for light by day and the fixed order of the moon and the stars for light by night, who stirs up the sea so that its waves roar, 'If this fixed order departs from before Me, then the offspring of Israel also will cease from being a nation before Me forever. If the heavens above can be measured and the foundations of the earth searched out below, then I will also cast off all the offspring of Israel ....'"

Throughout history there have been those who have sought to harm the Jews. In the course of time God has dealt with them in accordance with His promises to His people.

PART THREE

THE DELIVERANCE ATTAINED BY GOD'S PEOPLE

ESTHER 8:1–10:3

CHAPTER FOURTEEN

THE DELIVERANCE OF GOD'S PEOPLE

ESTHER 8:1–10:3

Xerxes (Ahasuerus) had graciously listened to Queen Esther as she recounted to him Haman's plot to exterminate all the Jews throughout the empire. Haman's actions with the queen had confirmed her accusation, and Xerxes had ordered his execution. But a "sword" still hung over the heads of all Jews in the 127 provinces. How may the intended calamity be averted?

An Unexpected Reward, 8:1-2

As Xerxes' anger cooled his thoughts focused, not on the danger facing the Jews, but how to reward Esther for drawing this matter to his attention. In the East felonious acts result in the forfeiture of property to the crown.[1] The same day Haman was executed Xerxes gave his property to Queen Esther. It was a munificent gift, for Haman was very rich! And Esther had Mordecai manage the estate for her.

Esther also brought Mordecai before King Xerxes. She told him that Mordecai was her cousin, and that he had

---

1. Josephus, *Antiquities of the Jews*, XII:1. See also Herodotus, *The Histories*, III:128-29.

cared for her after her parents died. Mordecai, of course, was much older and wiser than Esther, and that made his guardianship of her much more valuable.

Xerxes knew that Mordecai was a man of impeccable integrity with remarkable administrative gifts. He was also aware of the fact that he had previously rendered eminent service to the crown. As a result he did not hesitate to appoint Mordecai his new vizier to fill the vacancy left by Haman.

A Timely Decree, 8:3-14

As interesting as these events are, all the Jews throughout the empire still were under the sentence of death. What could be done to reverse Haman's edict? Esther realized that she must once again step into the breach and try to avert the danger facing her people. But how? Xerxes had already shown his magnanimity toward her; might a second appeal cause him to think that she was taking advantage of his kindness?

The danger of presuming too much on the king's favor was very real, and that is why when Esther again approached him she fell at his feet weeping. Her obvious grief gave added weight to her request that he put an end to the evil plan that Haman had devised.

Xerxes extended the gold scepter to her as a token that he was prepared to hear her request. As Esther rose and stood before him, her words were tactful and discrete. She did not presume on their relationship, nor remind him of his indebtedness to her for disclosing the plot to assassinate him. She was utterly sincere as she acknowledged his sovereignty. Her words, "If it please the king ..." show her respect. And her submission to his authority is again evident when she added, "and if he thinks it the right thing to do...." Only then did she implore him to save her people by overruling the decree that Haman had drafted.

The conduct of Esther in this matter was characterized by selflessness and a willing acceptance of whatever Xerxes may decide. The variety of expressions by which she described her relationship to her husband endeared him to her, and the way in which she placed all the blame for the planned massacre on Haman indicate her wisdom and knowledge of human nature.

Esther's appeal brought a positive response from the king. He said, "Now you write to the Jews as you see fit, in the king's name, and seal it with the king's signet ring; for a decree which is written in the name of the king and sealed with the king's signet ring may not be revoked" (8:8).

So the king's scribes were again called, this time on the twenty-third day of the third month (Sivan), and a new decree was written in accordance with all that Mordecai dictated. It was addressed "to all Jews, in all 127 provinces; according to their script and their language, as well as to the satraps, the governors and the princes of the provinces which extended from India to Ethiopia--to every province according to its script, and to all people according to their language" (8:9).

Mordecai sealed each dispatch with a seal bearing the impress of the king's signet ring. The letters were then sent by couriers on the fastest horses from the king's stable (8:15). This new decree gave the Jews who were in each and every city the right to assemble and to defend themselves. Taking words from Haman's letter they were given the right "to destroy, to kill and to annihilate" the entire army of any people or province which might attack them. Those under the ban included women and children. Furthermore, the Jews could legally appropriate the spoil of their enemies.

To give everyone fair warning, a copy of the edict was published in every province. The Jews could now make provision so as to be ready to protect themselves.

The Rejoicing of the Jews, 8:15-17

Meanwhile, in Susa Mordecai was honored by King Xerxes by being clothed in a gown woven of blue and white silk–the royal colors–and given a turban of gold cloth.[2] This attire immediately identified him as one whom the king delights to honor, and it made known to the people the high office to which he has been elevated. It is also interesting to note that the people were not commanded to prostrate themselves before their new grand vizier. Apparently they already held Mordecai in high esteem.

---

2. The word crown in this verse differs from the words used in 1:11; 2:17; and 6:8.

Meanwhile, the Jews throughout the empire realized the magnitude of their deliverance and gave expression to their feelings with glad rejoicing (contra. 4:3). And many people became proselytes to Judaism. Dr. C. F. Keil has pointed out that most of those who embraced Judaism did so out of the conviction that the religion of the Jews was superior to all other beliefs.[3]

A Triumph of the Jews, 9:1-19

Napoleon believed that God was on the side of the largest army. Had he reflected on the history of warfare he would have seen that the size of Xerxes' army did not guarantee the Persians victory over the Greeks in the Battles of Salamis and Plataea. Scripture assures us that "the Lord is not restrained to save by many or by few" (1 Samuel 14:6), and we have an example of His power to save in this chapter.

As the decree of Mordecai is read in every marketplace and town square of every city and village, the people fear that they will not be able to stand against the Jews. And all the nobles of the provinces, the satraps, the governors and the king's administrators help the Jews defend themselves because the fame of Mordecai and his reputation has spread rapidly throughout the empire.

The day of the intended massacre finally dawned. It had been identified by lot many months earlier. Now, however, the tables have been turned, and the people are about

---

3. Keil, *Esther*, 371.

to learn a very important lesson, *viz., those who try to destroy the Jews will themselves be destroyed.* Years earlier God had said to His people, "Those who plunder you will be plundered; all who make spoil of you I will despoil" (Jeremiah 30:16). The enemies of the Jews, envious of their wealth and success, hoped to destroy them and take their riches for themselves. Instead, they were destroyed.[4]

God's people were outnumbered by their enemies, but the majority of the Persians refused to fight them. Those who did take up arms against the Jews were resoundingly defeated. In a single day's fighting a significantly large number of people in all the provinces of the empire were killed.[5] And in Susa, the ten sons of Haman, who had their own residences, were also killed.[6]

The biblical writer emphasizes the fact that the Jews fought only against those men who fought against them. He also emphasizes the fact that they did *not* take the spoil that might legitimately have been theirs (9:10, 15-16). As with their forefather Abraham, they did not want it said that the

---

4. C f. McConville, *Ezra, Nehemiah, and Esther*, 193.
5. On the day set aside for the extermination of the Jews many of their enemies in Susa adroitly concealed themselves. Esther was compelled to ask the king to extend the decree by an additional day. This has exposed her to the charge of being actuated by a cruel and vindictive disposition, but this accusation is not necessarily accurate for we do not know the reasons for her request.
6. Patton, *The Book of Esther*, 284.

THE DELIVERANCE OF GOD'S PEOPLE

plunder of their enemies had made them rich (cf. Genesis 14:23).

Apparently Xerxes was indifferent to the number of deaths inflicted by the Jews, and asked Esther what more she wanted (9:11-12). She asked only that the sons of Haman be hanged (presumably in some public place) and that the purge be allowed to continue for another day (9:13-15). Permission was granted, and those enemies who had deliberately hidden themselves shared in the fate of those who had openly taken up arms against God's people.

The Feast of Purim, 9:20-32

To commemorate their unique deliverance the Jews celebrated their success with a feast. In the provinces they celebrated on the fourteenth of the month Adar, and in Susa on the fifteenth day of the same month. The festivities were marked by giving gifts and food to one another. And the Feast of Purim (from *pur* "to cast a lot") is still celebrated to this day.

Purim is not to be confused with the other feasts appointed by the Lord God (cf. Leviticus 23:1-44, e.g., *Passover* and *Unleavened Bread* that celebrated God's deliverance of Israel from slavery in Egypt; *First Fruits* that served as an occasion to praise God for giving them a bountiful harvest; *Weeks* or *Pentecost* that gave the Jews the opportunity to present to the Lord a new grain offering; the *Feast of Trumpets* that heralded the beginning of the new civil year; the *Day of Atonement* that marked the occasion when the sins of the nation were atoned for; and *Booths* or

Tabernacles that celebrated their deliverance from Egypt and God's provision of their needs throughout their wilderness wanderings).

The Feast of Purim was not given to the Jews by God (cf. 9:20-21), and is more akin to our Fourth of July. During the celebration of Purim the Book of Esther is read in its entirety, and in this way they are reminded of their deliverance from those who hated them.

The Greatness of Mordecai, 10:1-3

The Book of Esther closes with a tax imposed on the people by Xerxes. The phrase "laid a tribute on the land and on the sea" is used specifically to designate isles of the Mediterranean and the western countries visited by the Phoenicians. The money was probably needed to pay for his disastrous expedition against Greece.

Then there is a fine tribute to Mordecai: "And all the accomplishments of his authority and strength, and the full account of the greatness of Mordecai to which the king advanced him, are they not written in the Book of the Chronicles of the Kings of Media and Persia? For Mordecai the Jew was second only to King Ahasuerus, and great among the Jews and in favor with his many kinsmen, one who sought the good of his people and one who spoke for the welfare of his whole nation" (10:2-3).

Scripture states that the person who humbles himself will be exalted (Matthew 23:12), and Mordecai, who had sat contentedly at the kings gate, was raised to a position where he was second only to the king. He acted uniformly on the great principles of truth and righteousness, and all the people prospered.

The providence of God is plainly traceable in all the steps that led to his unexpected advancement; and though in the whole of this episode there is no extraordinary manifestation of God's power, no particular cause or agent that was in its working advanced above the ordinary pitch of nature, yet the outcome is in itself more admirable than if the same end had been effected by means that were truly miraculous. And while Mordecai's administration was conducted with a mild and impartial hand, he showed a peculiarly warm and friendly feeling to all his countrymen.

POST SCRIPT

Mordecai was the power behind the throne from this time to end of Xerxes' reign.. We know this, for in 465 B.C. another man occupied this office. Mordecai's ability and faithfulness touched everything he did, and he stands out as an example of an honesty and integrity in a corrupt system.

We do not know when Esther finished her earthly pilgrimage. If she outlived Xerxes she would have been given a place in the harem of the new king. The fact that he was the son of Vashti, and that Esther had replaced his mother, may have inclined him to be less than gracious to her. On the other hand the passing of time, coupled with Esther's quiet, winsome ways may have secured a reasonably place for her in the palace of Artaxerxes.

Xerxes was murdered in 465 B.C. A conspiracy was hatched by the sons of his deposed wife. They assassinated their father and Xerxes' son, Artaxerxes (whi reigned 465-424 B.C., who was born around 486 B.C.), was placed on the throne by his older brother.

The renowned Oxford historian, George Rawlinson, states that "the character of Xerxes falls below that of any preceding monarch. Excepting that he was not wholly devoid of a certain magnanimity, which made him listen patiently to those who opposed his views or gave him unpalatable advice,[7] and prevented him from exacting vengeance on some occasions.[8] Overall, he had scarcely a trait whereon the mind can rest with any satisfaction. Weak and easily led,[9] puerile in his gusts of passion and his complete abandonment of himself to them,[10] [he was] selfish, fickle, boastful, cruel, superstitious, licentious. He exhibits to us the Oriental despot in the most contemptible of all aspects, that wherein the moral and the intellectual qualities are equally defective. Seen in its entirety, Xerxes' career was one of unvarying vice and folly."[11]

And so the Book of Esther comes to a close.

---

7. Herodotus, *The Histories*, VII:105, 237; VIII:69.
8. Ibid., VII:136.
9. Ibid., VII:5-7, 12, 18; IX:109.
10. Ibid., VII:35, 45, 212, 238; VIII:90.
11. Rawlinson, *The Five Great Monarchies of the Ancient Eastern World*, III:4570-71.

www.ingramcontent.com/pod-product-compliance
Lightning Source LLC
Chambersburg PA
CBHW051926160426
43198CB00012B/2062